Speaking of the Devil

The Works of Satan

John M. Karstetter

Note: The majority of Scriptural references in this book are taken from the *World English Bible (WEB)*. The *World English Bible* is a modern translation of the *1901 American Standard Version*. It has been edited to conform to the *Greek Majority Text New Testament*. *WEB* has been placed in the Public Domain, which sets it apart from other revisions of the *ASV*, like the *New American Standard Bible* and the *Revised Standard Version*. Many Christians consider the *1901 American Standard* and the *King James Version* to be the most accurate Bibles available. The translation of *WEB* is faithful throughout to both versions. For more information on the *World English Bible*, go to worldenglishbible.org.

Copyright © 2018 John M. Karstetter
All rights reserved.
ISBN: 1984958542
ISBN-13: 978-1984958549

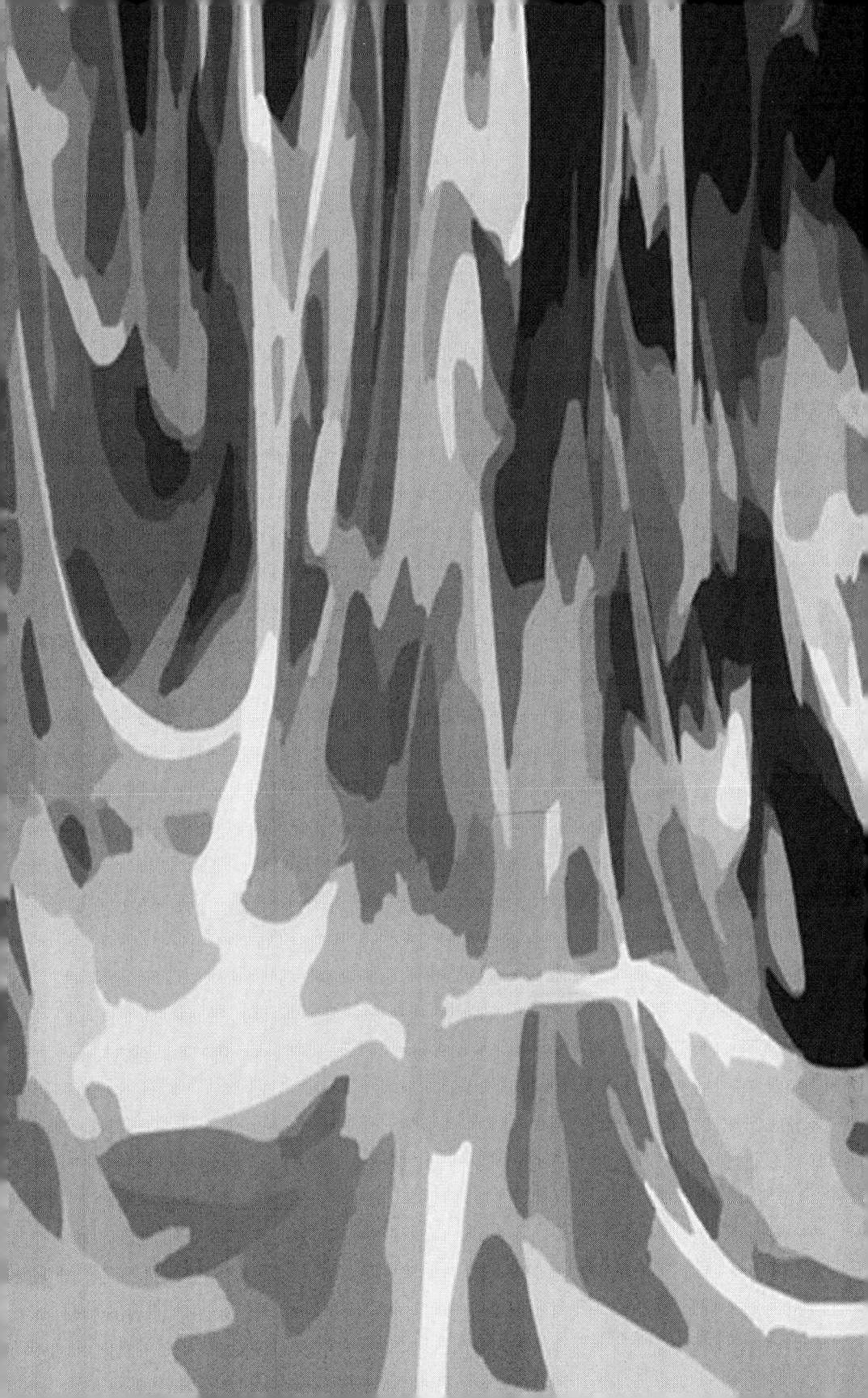

CONTENTS

WHY A BOOK ABOUT THE DEVIL? vii
HE IS KNOWN BY MANY NAMES 11
HE IS CALLED LUCIFER 17
PREACHER OF ETERNAL DAMNATION 27
DEVIL'S FAITH IS IN VAIN 37
THE DEVIL AND HIS DEMONS CONFESS GOD ... 41
ALL IN THE FAMILY 45
MIRACLES OR MAGICIANS 53
THE DEVIL IS A FAILURE 57
SATAN AND DEMONS OBEY GOD AND CHRIST .. 65
THE MASTER COUNTERFEITER 71
NINE HEAVENS 75
THE SNAKE 81
BEST MAN 85
BEST HEAVEN 91
MAN CAN BE BLESSED BY SATAN 95
THE DEVIL MADE ME DO IT 103
WHERE DID SATAN COME FROM 109
SEVEN TREES OF LIFE 113
VICTORY OVER SATAN—SALVATION 119
WHO IS JOHN KARSTETTER? 133

WHY A BOOK ABOUT THE DEVIL?

When we talk around the dinner table or at the office about what is happening in today's world, we often hear that trite expression, "This old world is going to hell in a hand basket!" Who knows where this phrase originated, but it has probably been used in every generation for eons. There is a rock song titled "Highway to Hell". Whether it be in a "hand basket" or on a "highway", this world is quickly headed in that direction!

Every person with any type of electronic device, be it a cell phone or a 60-inch flat screen, is bombarded daily with news that is worse than the day before. Terrorist groups are striking at will across the globe. There are mass shootings in churches and schools. Our law enforcement officers are not safe anymore even though they are heavily armed and highly trained. We had never heard of someone walking up to a parked police unit and executing an officer without warning, until now! It is no longer safe for us to shop at our local mall or leisurely walk through a public parking lot anymore. Who would have ever thought that today we would need to carry a concealed handgun when attending church!

Why is all of this happening on a daily basis? The answer is very simple...The EVIL ONE! Satan is alive and well in this world and is "hell bent" on going about his business. He has been tempting mankind since the Garden of Eden and will continue to do so until he is defeated on that final judgment day!

1 Peter 5:8 may be the most compelling verse in the Bible warning us about the Devil...

> "Be sober and self-controlled. Be watchful. Your adversary, the devil, walks around like a roaring lion, seeking whom he may devour."

We have either forgotten or simply ignore this deadly mistake in our everyday lives, until it is everlastingly too late!

When we stand before the judgment seat of Christ, and ALL of us will, will we want to hear this as our final verdict?

> "Not everyone who says to me, 'Lord, Lord,' will enter into the Kingdom of Heaven; but he who does the will of my Father who is in heaven. Many will tell me in that day, 'Lord, Lord, didn't we prophesy in your name, in your name cast out demons, and in your name do many mighty works?' Then I will tell them, 'I never knew you. Depart from me, you who work iniquity." (Matthew 7:21-23)

And this Departure will be for eternity!

This Scripture-filled book presents a unique study of Satan. You will be given facts that may change your mind about him and the way he operates in our lives. Some things you thought you knew about this enemy of God and man may not be so! No one can understand God,

Christ, the Holy Spirit, the Bible, the Church of the New Testament, and the Plan of Salvation until we understand the Devil and why we have this nemesis in our lives.

The intent is to present evidence from the Bible, God's Inspired Word, that Satan is *real*, yesterday and today. Satan and the Devil are synonymous with all the other names he is called in the Bible. He assumes countless disguises in his attempts to deceive mankind.

We must continually *be aware of* and *on the defense for* his "deadly" deception! As commanded in Scripture, we are to arm ourselves to daily resist the never-ending attack from the "Evil One". The apostle Paul strongly admonishes us...

> "Finally, be strong in the Lord, and in the strength of his might. Put on the whole armor of God, that you may be able to stand against the wiles of the devil. For our wrestling is not against flesh and blood, but against the principalities, against the powers, against the world's rulers of the darkness of this age, and against the spiritual forces of wickedness in the heavenly places. Therefore put on the whole armor of God, that you may be able to withstand in the evil day, and, having done all, to stand. Stand therefore, having the utility belt of truth buckled around your waist, and having put on the breastplate of righteousness, and having fitted your feet with the preparation of the Good News of peace; above all, taking up the shield of faith, with which you will be able to quench all the fiery darts of the evil one. And take the helmet of salvation, and the sword of the Spirit, which is the word of God; with all prayer and requests, praying at all times in the Spirit, and being watchful to this end in all

perseverance and requests for all the saints."
(Ephesians 6:10-18)

Paul is speaking of spiritual armor here; however, today it takes on a dual meaning in our physical protection against evil doers of Satan on this earth!

We as Christians shall defeat this *ENEMY*, if we remain faithful to the end of our battle upon this earth, through the blood, grace, and mercy of our Lord and Savior, Jesus Christ.

Get ready to learn about the *EVIL ONE:*
> *He is Known by Many Names*
> *He is Called Lucifer*
> *Preacher of Eternal Damnation*
> *Devil's Faith is in Vain*
> *The Devil and His Demons Confess God*
> *All in the Family*
> *Miracles or Magicians*
> *The Devil is a Failure*
> *Satan and Demons Obey God and Christ*
> *The Master Counterfeiter*
> *Nine Heavens*
> *The Snake*
> *Best Man*
> *Best Heaven*
> *Blessed by Satan*
> *The Devil Made Me Do It*
> *Where Did Satin Come From*
> *Seven Trees of Life*
> *Victory Over Satan – Salvation*

Chapter 1

HE IS KNOWN BY MANY NAMES

In the sales profession, you must know all about the products you sell. Each customer has different wants and needs. To be successful in presenting and selling any product, you have to know your customer's "hot buttons". Equally important, you are required to know the strengths and weaknesses of your competitor's products as well.

This same concept can be applied to our spirituality. To please God, we must know what is required of us through the study of His Word throughout our lives while here on this earth. Since Satan is the enemy of God and mankind and is continually in competition with Him, we must study the Devil to see how he works in our lives to be able to overcome his temptations. It is imperative that we know his *"strengths"* and always be aware of our *"weaknesses!"* This study will begin with his "names" in both the Old and New Testaments.

Old Testament Names
- Anointed Guardian Cherub (Ezekiel 28:14)
- Belial (Deuteronomy 13:13; Judges 19:22-30; 1 Samuel 1:16; 1 Samuel 2:12; 1 Samuel 10:27; 1 Samuel 25:25; 2 Samuel 23:6; 1 Kings 21:10; 1 Kings 21:13)
- Devils (Leviticus 17:7; Deuteronomy 32:17; 2 Chronicles 1:15; Psalm 106:37)
- Evil Spirits (Judges 9:23; 1 Samuel 16:14-16; 1 Samuel 16:23; 1 Samuel 18:10; 1 Samuel 19:9-10)
- Leviathan (Isaiah 27:1)
- Little Horn (Daniel 8:9-12)
- Lucifer (Isaiah 14:12-14, see Chapter 2)
- Lying Spirits (1 Kings 22:22-35; 2 Chronicles 18:20-34)
- Satan (2 Samuel 24:1; 1 Chronicles 21:1; Job 1:6; Job 1:7; Job 1:8; Job 1:9-11; Job 1:12; Job 1:12; Job 2:1-7)
- Serpent (Genesis 3:1, 4-5, 14-15; Romans 16:20)

New Testament Names
- Abaddon (Revelation 9:11)
- Accuser of Our Brethren (Revelation 12:10)
- Adversary (1 Timothy 5:14; 1 Peter 5:8)
- Ancient Serpent (Revelation 12:9; Revelation 20:10)
- Angel of the Abyss (Revelation 9:11)
- Apollyon (Revelation 9:11)
- Beast (Revelation 14:9-10)

SPEAKING OF THE DEVIL

- Beelzebub (KJV) Or Beelzebul (World English Bible Version) (Matthew 10:25; Matthew 12:24, 27; Luke 11:15-19; Mark 3:22)
- Belial (2 Corinthians 6:15)
- Chief of Devils (Luke 11:15)
- Deceiver (Revelation 12:9)
- Devil (Matthew 4:1; Matthew 4:5-6, 8-9, 11; Matthew 9:32-33; Matthew 11:18; Matthew 12:22; Matthew 13:39; Matthew 15:22; Matthew 17:14-18; Matthew 25:41; Mark 1:13; Mark 5:15,18; Mark 7:26; Mark 7:29-30; Luke 4:2-11,13, 33-35; Luke 7:33; Luke 8:12, 29; Luke 9:42; Luke 11:14; John 6:70; John 7:20; John 8:44, 48-49, 52; John 10:20-21; John 13:2; Acts 10:38; Acts 13:10; Ephesians 4-27, 6:11; 1 Timothy 3:6-7; 2 Timothy 2:26; Hebrews 2:14; James 4:7;1 Peter 5:8; 1 John 3:8, 10; Jude 1:9 Revelation 2:10; Revelation 12:7,12; Revelation 20:1-3)
- Devils (Matthew 4:24; Matthew 8:16,28-29,31,33; Matthew 9:34; Matthew 10:8; Matthew 12:27-28; Mark 1:32, 39; Mark 3:15; Mark 6:13; Mark 3:22; Mark 5:12; Mark 9:38; Luke 4:41; Luke 8:2,27,31,33,36-36,38; Luke 9:1,49; Luke 10:17; Luke 11:15,18-20; Luke 13:32; 1 Corinthians 10:20 1 Corinthians 10:21; 1 Timothy 4:1; James 2:19; Revelation 9:20; Revelation 18:2)
- Dragon (Revelation 12:4,7,13,16-17; Revelation 13:2,4,11; Revelation 20:2)
- Dumb Spirit (Mark 9:17)
- Enemy (Matthew 13:25, 28, 39; Timothy 5:14)
- Evil One (John 17:15)

- Evil Spirits (Luke 7:21; Luke 8:2; Acts 19:1213, 15-16)
- Father (John 8:41, 44-45)
- Father of Lies (John 8:44)
- Foul Spirit (Mark 9:25; Revelation 18:2)
- Gates of Hell (Matthew 16:18)
- God of This World (2 Corinthians 4:4)
- Great Dragon (Revelation 12:9)
- Great Red Dragon (Revelation 12:3-4)
- Iniquity (2 Thessalonians 2:7)
- Lawless One (2 Thessalonians 2:8-10)
- Legion (Mark 5:9-10; Luke 8:30)
- Liar (John 8:44)
- Mammon (Matthew 6:24; Luke 16:9, 11-16)
- Murderer (John 8:44)
- Perdition (John 17:12; 2 Thessalonians 2:3)
- Power of Darkness (Colossians 1:13)
- Prince of Devils (Matthew 9:34; Matthew 12:24; Mark 3:22)
- Prince of the Power of The Air (Ephesians 2:2)
- Prince of This World (John 12:31; John 14:30; John 16:11)
- Rulers of Darkness (Ephesians 6:12)
- Ruler of Demons (Luke 11:15)
- Roaring Lion (1 Peter 5:8)
- Satan (Matthew 4:10; Matthew 12:26; Matthew 16:23; Mark 3:23, 26; Mark 8:33; Luke 10:18 See Chapter 2; Luke 11:18; Luke 13:16; Luke 22:3, 31; John 13:27; Acts 5:3; Acts 26:18; Roman 16:20; 1 Corinthians 5:5; 1 Corinthians 7:2-5; 2 Corinthians 2:11; 2 Corinthians 11:14; 2 Corinthians 12:7; 1 Thessalonians 2:18; 2

Thessalonians 2:9; 1 Timothy 1:20; 1 Timothy 5:15; Revelation 2:9; Revelation 3:9; Revelation 2:13-14, 24; Revelation 12:9; Revelation 20:2, 7-8)
- Seducing Spirits (1 Timothy 4:1)
- Serpent (2 Corinthians 11:3; Revelation 12:15)
- Spirits (Matthew 8:16; Matthew 12:45; Mark 9:20,26; Luke 4:33-34; Luke 9:39, 54-55; Luke 10:20; Luke 11:26; James 4:5; 1 John 4:1-3, 6)
- Spirits of the Devil (Revelation 16:14)
- Spirit of Divination (Acts 16:16,18)
- Spirit of Infirmity (Luke 13:11)
- Spiritual Wickedness in High Places (Ephesians 6:12)
- Spirit That Works in the Children of Disobedience (Ephesians 2:2)
- Tempter (Matthew 4:1; 1 Thessalonians 3:5)
- Thief (John 10:10)
- Unclean Spirit(s) (Matthew 12:43-45; Mark 1:23-24; Mark 5:2-5,7-8,13; Mark 1:26-27; Mark 3:11,30; Mark 6:7; Mark 7:25; Luke 4:36; Luke 6:18; Luke 8:28; Luke 9:42; Luke 11:24-26; Acts 5:16; Revelation 16:13)
- Wicked (Ephesians 6:16; 2 Thessalonians 2:8)
- Wicked One (Matthew 13:19; Matthew 13:38; Ephesians 6:16)

It is interesting to note that all these names of the Devil are mentioned in both the Old and New Testaments, except one. *Lying Spirit* is only found in the New Testament.

We need strength daily to resist each one of these names. (See Ephesians 6:10-18.)

Chapter 2

HE IS CALLED LUCIFER

One of the most common misconceptions among Bible believers is that Satan is also referred to as "Lucifer" in Scripture. We even have a television show today titled this name. Who knows when this deception began, but we certainly know the source...The Devil! What is the origin of the name Lucifer, what is its meaning, and is it a synonym for "The Devil"? Let's see what the Bible tells us about his being identified as Lucifer.

The name Lucifer is only mentioned *one* time in the Bible. You will find it in Isaiah 14:12, *King James Version*:

> "How art thou fallen from heaven, O Lucifer, son of the morning! how art thou cut down to the ground, which didst weaken the nations!"

This is the first attempt to prove that Satan once lived in God's heavenly home, that he was once righteous, then sinned and was cast out of that heaven. Verse 12 does *not* refer to Satan at all, but instead to the *king of Babylon,* most likely Nebuchadnezzar II.

The Hebrew word translated "Lucifer" is *helel* or *heylele,* meaning "to shine" or "to bear light". However, the King James Bible translators did not translate *helel* as Lucifer because of something inherent in the Hebrew term itself. The term was describing the planet Venus, employed the Latin term "Lucifer" or light-bearing to designate "the morning star", the planet Venus.

Let's break down Chapter 14, verse by verse, to prove that the Devil and Lucifer were not the same personality, as he was the King of Babylon.

Starting with verse four... "that thou shalt take up this proverb against the King of Babylon, and say, How hath the oppressor ceased! the golden city ceased!" *King of Babylon is plainly the "oppressor of his people".*

Verse five: "The Lord hath broken the staff of the wicked, *and* the scepter of the rulers". *Staff and scepter of this King.*

Verse six: "He who smote the people in wrath with a continual stroke, he that ruled the nations in anger, is persecuted, *and* none hindereth". *This King smote, ruled, and persecuted his people, while no one stopped him.*

Verse seven: "The whole earth is at rest, and is quiet: they break forth into singing". *They are at rest and break out in song when this angry King falls!*

Verse eight: "Yea, the fir trees rejoice at thee, *and* the cedars of Lebanon, *saying,* since thou art laid down, no feller [*lumberjack*] is come up against us". *The King has been overthrown, thus no one comes to cut the cedars down and his people are at peace.*

Verse nine: "Hell from beneath is moved for thee to meet *thee* at thy coming: it stirreth up the dead for thee, *even* all the chief ones of the earth; it hath raised up from their thrones all the kings of the nations". *This King has died, those in hell anxiously await for him to arrive.*

Verse ten: "All they shall speak and say unto thee, Art thou also become weak as we? art thou become like unto us"? *This terrible King has lost his power, he is no Lucifer!*

Verse eleven: "Thy pomp is brought down to the grave, *and* the noise of thy viols *harps*: the worm is spread under thee, and the worms cover thee". *This King of Babylon is not Lucifer, as he was flesh and blood and is now being eaten by worms.*

Verse twelve: "How art thou fallen from heaven, O Lucifer, son of the morning! *how* art thou cut down to the ground, which didst weaken the nations!" *This same King, this same Lucifer fallen from heaven? Not God's heavenly home! But cut down to the ground, having weakened nations on this earth, not heaven. He had exalted himself only to fall into a grave, eaten by worms.*

Verse thirteen: "For thou hast said in thine heart, I will ascend into heaven, I will exalt my throne above the stars of God: I will sit also upon the mount of the congregation, in the sides of the north" *Instead of this "Lucifer" coming down from heaven, since this King was on earth, he brags that he will ascend into heaven.*

Verse fourteen: "I will ascend above the heights of the clouds; I will be like the most High". *This King was under the clouds, again bragging that he would be like the Most High.*

Verse fifteen: "Yet thou shalt be brought down to

hell, to the sides of the pit". *This so-called Lucifer is to be brought down to hell, like the Devil!*

Verses sixteen and seventeen: "They that see thee shall narrowly look upon thee, and consider thee, saying, Is this the man that made the earth to tremble, that did shake kingdoms; That made the world as a wilderness, and destroyed the cities thereof; that opened not the house of his prisoners"? *This King of Babylon is a "man", not Lucifer. He caused the "earth" to tremble with his wickedness, destroyed his wilderness and cities, and would not even open his house of prisoners.*

This King of Babylon was surely a cruel ruler, living on this earth, certainly not Lucifer! We learn that he was a "man"! His desire was to ascend into heaven to be above God. He was then sent to the deepest, darkest depths of shame and disgrace. His body was eaten of worms in the grave.

Christ told mankind that no "man", and this King of Babylon was certainly a man, not Lucifer: "No one has ascended into heaven, but he who descended out of heaven, the Son of Man, who is in heaven".

Another common misconception about seeing Satan fall from heaven is the "Seventy". First of all, who were the Seventy? The seventy disciples or seventy apostles were early messengers of Jesus mentioned only in the Gospel of Luke. Jesus appointed them and sent them out in pairs on a specific mission, which is detailed in the text.

> "The seventy returned with joy, saying, 'Lord, even the demons are subject to us in your name!' He said to them, 'I saw Satan having fallen like lightning from heaven." (Luke 10:17-18)

Here is another reference in an effort to prove that the Devil was once a citizen in God's heavenly home, but still does not prove this point. It does prove that the Devil fell under the preaching of the seventy in this Scripture. But consider this, if it was from God's heavenly home, it would also prove that Satan was not on this earth during the time God placed him in the Garden of Eden and all the years the Bible documents his tempting mankind. God's Word also mentions "other heavens". One of Satan's names is the "Prince of the Air", thus, he fell from his home in the physical heaven or great space surrounding this earth as a result of the preaching of the Seventy. This is one of several heavens that will be discussed in another chapter. The Devil not only fell from the preaching of the Seventy, he continues to fall to this day as God's Word continues to be preached.

Since Satan set foot in the Garden of Eden, he has always been at war with mankind. So the question is, which heaven does he war? Scripture reveals *nine* different heavens which will also be discussed in a later chapter. The Apostle Paul spoke of a "third heaven" in 2 Corinthians 12:2.

David of the Old Testament speaks of "heavens of heavens" in Psalms 148:4. We are used to thinking when heaven is mentioned it always refers to God's heavenly home; however, that is not so.

The Devil has been at war with God and mankind since he appeared in the Garden of Eden. This proves that he did not come from or war in God's heavenly home, so again, where does he war with man today? Revelation 11:15 tells us:

> "The seventh angel sounded, and great voices in heaven followed, saying, 'The kingdom of the world has become the Kingdom of our Lord, and of his Christ. He will reign forever and ever!'"

There is our answer, the kingdoms of *this world*, and not the kingdoms of *God's Home* world? The voices heard in that heaven were on the earth, not above!

Revelation 11:19 tells us that God's temple that is in heaven was opened, and the ark of the Lord's covenant was seen in his temple. Lightnings, sounds, thunders, an earthquake, and great hail followed. It describes what could only happen on earth: lightnings, thunders, great hail, and earthquakes.

It has been long preached in error that the Devil was once in God's heavenly home above, that he warred with God up there. He was defeated, then cast out and down to the earth ready to tempt man as soon as he was created. It simply did not happen that way.

The Bible provides more proof in the following:

> "There was war in the sky. Michael and his angels made war on the dragon. The dragon and his angels made war. They didn't prevail, neither was a place found for him any more in heaven. The great dragon was thrown down, the old serpent, he who is called the Devil and Satan, the deceiver of the whole world. He was thrown down to the earth, and his angels were thrown down with him." (Revelation 12:7-9)

You would think this Scripture teaches that the Devil was once in God's heavenly home above. It would also indicate that he was cast out into the earth and was to fulfill God's work for him to tempt man with his first appearance upon earth.

The Church is an elevated Institution that extends up to God Himself.

Isaiah 2:2 describes it as the mountain of Yahweh's house that shall be established on the top of the mountains and shall be raised above the hills; and all nations shall flow to it. We speak now of the Church-heaven which is down here in the earthly realm from which Satan was cast out. All of the heavens will be identified and discussed in a later chapter.

Now back to the description of this war in heaven. Beginning in Revelation 12:10-11, we read (italics are author's comment):

> "I heard a loud voice in heaven, saying, 'Now the salvation, *Did people need to be saved in God's heavenly home?*, and the power, and the Kingdom of our God, and the authority of His Christ; *was Christ showing salvation for those there in God's heaven,* for the accuser of our brothers, *did they have a brotherhood up there too?*, has been thrown down, who accuses them before our God day and night', *the brethren up there stand accused?*"
>
> They overcame him because of the Lamb's blood, and because of the word of their testimony. They didn't love their life, even to death, *proving this war was on the earth with the shedding of His blood*, and by the Word of their testimony, preaching of the Word, the Gospel, They didn't love their life, even to death. (Revelation 12:10-11)

They overcame Satan and his angels by doing three things. First, they overcame by the blood of the Lamb (Christ). *Christ had not been "crucified" yet, so it had to be here on this earth.* Second, they overcame the Devil by the Word of their testimony, *the "Word of God" being preached here.* Third, they were not concerned about their earthly lives even unto their own death! This shows they were mortal beings and could die in the flesh. So this war could not have been in heaven, as flesh and blood do not enter there; 1 Corinthians 15:50 so states.

It would also mean that sin and death did not originate in the Garden of Eden, but in God's heavenly home, which He would never have allowed to happen! (Revelation 21:27.)

We have another account of this "war in heaven", *this same heaven just mentioned.* (Again, italics are author's comment.)

> I saw the heaven opened, and behold, a white horse, and he who sat on it is called Faithful and True. In righteousness he judges, *not with a steel sword* and makes war, *in this heaven.* His eyes are a flame of fire, and on his head are many crowns. He has names written and a name written which no one knows but he himself. He is clothed in a garment sprinkled with blood, *this was an earthly war.* His name is called "The Word of God." The armies which are in heaven followed him on white horses, clothed in white, pure, fine linen. Out of his mouth proceeds a sharp, double-edged sword, God's Word-Ephesians 6:17, that with it He should strike the nations, *earthly nations.* He will rule them with an iron rod. He treads the wine press of the fierceness of the wrath of God, the Almighty, *this war was in progress.* He has on his garment and on his thigh a name written,

"KING OF KINGS, AND LORD OF LORDS." I saw an angel standing in the sun. He cried with a loud voice, saying to all the birds that fly in the sky, "Come! Be gathered together to the great supper of God, *those who died in this war are fed to the fowls, this earthly war*, that you may eat the flesh of kings, *again proving this war could not be in God's heaven, for no flesh and blood can enter there*, the flesh of captains, the flesh of mighty men, and the flesh of horses and of those who sit on them, and the flesh of all men, both free and slave, and small and great." I saw the beast, and the kings of the *earth*, and their armies, gathered together to make war against him who sat on the horse, and against His army, *earthly kings and armies are warring against Christ and his army, proving that his heaven has to be on this earth*. The beast was taken, and with him the false prophet who worked the signs in his sight, with which he deceived those who had received the mark of the beast, *which takes place on this earth*, and those who worshiped his image. These two were thrown alive into the lake of fire that burns with sulfur, *denotes victory for Christ and Christians in this war*. The rest were killed with the sword of him who sat on the horse, the sword which came out of his mouth. All the birds were filled with their flesh. (Revelation 19:11-21)

Revelation shows Christ being the Leader of Christians in this war with earthly kings, earthly armies and with the earthly false prophet. These verses prove that the "WAR IN HEAVEN", in the CHURCH, is over CHRIST trying to get Satan out of the lives of every possible church member. This war was never in God's heavenly home, nor was the Devil, but on this earth and continues to this day.

Revelation is the only book in the New Testament that focuses primarily on prophetic events written in Apocalyptic style. These visions and symbols are revealed to the Apostle John, the author of the Book of Revelation, during his exile on the island of Patmos, concerning the resurrected Christ, who alone has authority to judge the earth, to remake it and to rule it in righteousness.

Chapter 3

PREACHER OF ETERNAL DAMNATION

When we think of a "minister", we generally see that person as one who teaches and preaches the Word of God. These individuals are generally referred to as teachers, preachers, evangelists, pastors, priests, or rabbis.

The Devil works as a minister as well, except his goal is to lead people *away* from God. His "gospel is perverted" and he uses *any means* needed to accomplish his objective, which is to destroy our spiritual lives, our very souls!

Satan will be cast down to hell, and he is doing his best to take as many souls on this earth with him when he goes. The Bible tells us that he will be successful in taking many to that place of eternal damnation and suffering.

> "For *wide* is the gate and *broad* is the road *that leads to destruction*, and *many enter through it.*"
> Matthew 7:13

Let's take a look at how he and his demons operate to accomplish this end.

Old Testament Ministries
- The Serpent Enticed the Woman—She Falls for His Trickery. (Genesis 3:1-5)
- The Serpent Told Eve She Would Not Die. (Genesis 3:4-5)
- The Serpent Said the Woman Could Be God-Like. (Genesis 3:6-7)
- God Cursed the Serpent for His Deception. (Genesis 3:14-15)
- Satan Travels the Entire Earth, Seeking Those He May Deceive. (Job 2:2)
- Satan and God Talk About the Temptation of Job. (Job 1:8-12; Job 2:2-6)
- Satan Brags That He Will Make Job Deny God to His Face. (Job 2:4-5)
- Satan Destroys Job's Children and All of His Possessions. (Job 1:8-19)
- Satan Stands Before the Lord and His Angels. (Job 2:1)
- Satan Strikes Job with Sickness. (Job 2:7)
- Satan Stands Next to Judas By His Permission and Desire. (Psalm 109:6)
- Satan and His Demons are Worshiped. (Leviticus 17:7; Deuteronomy 32:17; 2 Chronicles 11:15; Psalm 106:37)
- Evil Spirits Trouble King Saul. (1 Samuel 16:12-16)
- Evil Spirit Tempting King Saul to Kill David. (1 Samuel 18:10-11)

New Testament Ministries
- The Devil Tempted Christ in the "Lust of The Flesh". (Matthew 4:1-3; Luke 4:1-3)
- He Tempted Christ in the "Pride of Life". (Matthew 4:5-6; Luke 4:9-11)
- The Devil Tempted Christ in the "Lust of The Eye". (Matthew 4:8-11; Luke 4:5-7)
- Christ Was Tempted for Forty Days. (Matthew 4:1-2)
- He Obeyed Christ When Ordered to Leave His Sight. (Matthew 4:10; Luke 4:13)
- He and His Demons Possess People. (Matthew 4:24; Matthew 8:16; Matthew 8:33; Mark 1:32; Mark 5:15; Mark 5:18; Luke 8:30-31; Luke 8:36)
- Demons Obeyed Christ When Commanded Leave People. (Matthew 8:16; Matthew 9:33-34)
- They Made People Fierce and to Live in the Tombs. (Matthew 8:28; Mark 5:2-5; Luke 8:27)
- Demons Prayed to Enter Swine. (Luke 8:32)
- They Cause People to Have No Ability to Speak. (Matthew 9:32-33; Matthew 12:22; Mark 9:25; Luke 11:14)
- Satan Rules Over Demons, He is Their Prince. (Matthew 9:34; Matthew 12:24; Mark 3:22)
- He Causes People to Become Blind and Not Able to Speak. (Matthew 12:22)
- He Snatches Away Truth-Seeds from The Hearts of Believers. (Matthew 13:19; Luke 8:12; Mark 4:15)
- The Devil Sows Weeds Among the Wheat. (Matthew 13:25, 28, 39)

- He Produces Children Called Weeds. (Matthew 13:38)
- He Causes People to Suffer. (Matthew 15:22; Luke 6:18; Acts 5:16)
- He Tries to Overcome the Church but Does Not Succeed. (Matthew 16:18)
- Satan Causes People to Go Insane. (Matthew 17:14-18; Mark 5:15; Mark 9:17-25)
- He is the Ruler Over the Wicked Angels. (Matthew 25:41)
- Jesus Did Not Want Satan's Demons to Know Who He Was. (Mark 1:34)
- Demons Obeyed the Apostles When Commanded to Leave People. (Matthew 10:8; Mark 3:15; Mark 6:7; Mark 6:13; Luke 9:1; Luke 10:20; Acts 16:18; Acts 19:12; Matthew 8:31-32; Mark 5:12-13; Luke 8:32-33)
- Demons Prayed Not to Be Sent Out of the Country. (Mark 5:9-10)
- They Possessed the Little Girl. (Mark 7:25)
- They Make People Have Convulsions. (Mark 9:25-26, 39)
- Demons Assaulted People Down. (Luke 4:35; Luke 9:42; Luke 8:2; Luke 9:42)
- Satan and His Demons Bound People with Chains. (Luke 8:29; Luke 13:16)
- Demons Begged Jesus Not to Send Them into the Abyss. (Luke 8:30-31)
- They Make People Cry and Convulse. (Luke 9:39)
- Demons Would Disguise Themselves. (Luke 9:55)
- Demons Obeyed the Seventy Disciples. (Luke 10:17, 20)

- Satan Falls from Heaven by the Preaching of the Truth. (Luke 10:18, See Chapter 2)
- Satan Entered Judas Causing Christ to Be Betrayed. (Luke 22:3; John 13:2, 27)
- Satan Tempted Simon To Do What He Wanted. (Luke 22:31)
- Demons Follow After Their Father Satan's Wicked Ways. (John 8:41, 44; Acts 13:10; 2 Thessalonians 2:3; 1 John 3:8,10)
- The Devil is a Murderer and a Liar. (John 8:44)
- Demons Enabled People to Be Fortune Tellers for Money. (Acts 16:16)
- Satan and His Demons Represent Darkness. (Acts 26:18)
- Satan Tempts People Thru the Sexual Duties of Their Marriage. (1 Corinthians 7:2-5; Exodus 21:10)
- They Receive Sacrifices from The Gentiles, God is Not Pleased. (1 Corinthians 10:20)
- They Counterfeit Both the "Cup and Table of the Lord". (1 Corinthians 10:21)
- Satan And His Demons Took Advantage of The People. (2 Corinthians 2:11)
- Satan Blinds the Minds of Unbelievers. (2 Corinthians 4:4)
- Satan Corrupted the Minds of People. (2 Corinthians 11:3)
- Satan Transforms Himself into An Angel of Light to Deceive. (2 Corinthians 11:14)
- Satan Transforms Himself into An Apostle of Christ. (2 Corinthians 11:13)
- He Masquerades His Servants as the Ministers

of Righteousness. (2 Corinthians 11:15)
- Satan Torments the Apostle Paul. (2 Corinthians 12:7)
- The Devil is Over the Power of the Air and Works in the Children of Disobedience. (Ephesians 2:2)
- We are to Guard Against His Trickery Through the Word of God. (Ephesians 6:11)
- He Wrestles Against People Through Spiritual Forces, Not Physical. (Ephesians 6:12)
- He Hurls Spiritual Fiery Darts Against Good People. (Ephesians 6:16)
- Satan is of Darkness and Uses That Power Against Us. (Colossians 1:13)
- Satan Does His Best to Discourage Preachers. (1 Thessalonians 2:18)
- Satan Always Causes Havoc in All That He Does. (2 Thessalonians 2:7)
- Satan and His False Prophets Work Miracles. (Matthew 24:24; Mark 13:22; 2 Thessalonians 2:9; Revelation 13:11-14; Revelation 16:14; Revelation 19:20)
- His Specialty is Working on New Converts to Christ. (1 Timothy 3:6)
- He Tries to Discourage Those Who Are Outside of the Realm. (1 Timothy 3:7)
- He Snares People as if They Are Animals. (2 Timothy 2:26)
- He Loves to Lure People Away from God's Word by False Doctrine. (1 Timothy 4:1; 1 Timothy 5:15)
- He Targets Young Widows in the Church, Encouraging Gossip. (Timothy 5:14)

- Satan Takes People Away, Until They Realize They Are in His Snare. (2 Timothy 2:26)
- He Can Exercise the Power of Physical Death. (Hebrews 2:14)
- Even His Devils Believe in God and Tremble. (James 2:19)
- They Lust to Envy Through His Temptations. (James 4:5)
- Satan Will Flee If We Resist Him. (James 4:7)
- He is Like a Roaring Lion Trying to Devour Us. (1 Peter 5:8)
- Satan Has Been Trying to Overcome Us from The Beginning. (1 John 2:13-14)
- Satan Has Been Sinning Since the Beginning. (John 3:8)
- Satan Tries to Deceive Us with False Teaching. (1 John 4:1)
- All Those Who Do Not Believe in God Are Antichrists of Satan. (1 John 4:3)
- False Teachers Error. (1 John 4:6)
- Satan Challenged Michael Over Dead Bodies of Good People. (Jude 1:9)
- Satan Has His Own Synagogues and Counterfeit Churches. (Revelation 2:9; 3:9)
- Satan Tries People by Casting Them into Prison. (Revelation 2:10)
- Satan Spreads False Doctrines in The Church. (Revelation 2:13-14, 24)
- Satan Is the Destroyer, As His Hebrew Name, Abaddon, And His Greek Name Apollyon Imply. (Revelation 9:11)
- Satan Was Worshiped by The Wicked.

(Revelation 9:20; Revelation 13:4)
- The Dragon Pulls Down Stars from The Church-Sky, And Was Ready to Devour Christ, The Woman's Child (Revelation 12:3-4)
- The Dragon and His Angels War in The Church-Heaven Against Christians In the Apostle John's Vision. (Revelation 12:7-11; Revelation 19:11-21)
- Satan Continually Deceives This World, His Main Weapon. (Revelation 12:9; 1 Timothy 2:14-15; Revelation 20:7-10)
- Satan Accuses the Brethren, But He Will Lose. (Revelation 12:10)
- Satan Knows He Has but Little Time to Work Against God. (Revelation 12:12)
- The Dragon Hates the Woman Who Has Given Birth to Christ. (Revelation 12:13)
- The Serpent Puts Up His Best Attempt to Drown the Woman. (Revelation 12:15)
- The Dragon Gives Up on The Woman and Moves On. (Revelation 12:17)
- The Dragon Gives Power to The Beast, His Best Effort to Do His Biddings. (Revelation 13:2)
- Satan And His Demons Occupy the Great Spiritual Babylon. (Revelation 18:2)
- Satan Tempts Christ With False Scripture. (Matthew 4:5-6)
- His Name Is the Prince of The World, Will Try to Take Over When Christ Ascends into Heaven. (John 14:30)
- The Devil Uses Idolatry and Does Worthless Work, The Meaning of His Name Belial. (2 Corinthians 6:15)

- Satan Is The "Lord of Dung", The Meaning Of "Beelzebub." (Matthew 12:24; Mark 3:22; Luke 11:15)
- He Corrupts Minds from Obeying the Simplicity of The Gospel. (2 Corinthians 11:3; Revelation 3:21)

Chapter 4

DEVIL'S FAITH IS IN VAIN

Does Satan and his demons have faith and believe in Jesus? Absolutely! They know and believe that He is the One and only Son of Almighty God.

However, even though they have faith, it does not, nor will it ever, save them.

THE DEVIL AND HIS DEMONS BELIEVE THAT JESUS CHRIST IS THE SON OF GOD. (Matthew 8:29; Mark 3:11; Luke 4:41; Romans 1:30)

THEY BELIEVE THAT JESUS IS THE SON OF THE MOST HIGH GOD. (Mark 5:7; Luke 8:28)

The devils know all about this doctrine of "gods many" and "lords many", man-made gods, but they believe that Jesus Christ is the Son of the most high God, and eternally put to shame the so-called "intellectuals" who deny the Deity of Christ. It is possible to be meaner than the Devil—denying Christ is worse.

DEVILS KNOW THAT HE IS JESUS OF NAZARETH. (Mark 1:24; Luke 4:34)

While wicked men are asking if "any good thing can some out of Nazareth", devils are telling the world that they believe in Christ and that he is of the city of Nazareth. Devils know far more about God than many of us know and some of them are not as malicious as some people—they believe in Christ while people deny Him.

DEVILS KNOW AND BELIEVE THAT HE IS THE HOLY ONE OF GOD. (Mark 1:24; Luke 1:24)

The devils believe that Jesus is Holy, that he is sinless and that is record that the Bible gives of Him. Therefore, heaven and hell testify together that Jesus never sinned and all the combined forces of this earth have not been able to put a finger upon a black spot in His wonderful life. If his enemies could find the least fault against Him, they would give wealth untold for it—they would publish it to the ends of the earth. Since the devils believe that Jesus Christ is the Son of God, is Jesus of Nazareth, is the HOLY ONE and that He is the "SON OF THE MOST HIGH GOD", we do maintain that any one that denies His Deity is more despicable that the devils.

SATAN, THE SERPENT-DEVIL BELIEVES IN THE TRUE AND LIVING GOD. (Genesis 3:1-5; Job 1:9-10)

Satan has frequent conversations with God and knows His works. He knows that He had hedged in Job and all that he had, showing again that he is not only a believer in God, but that he knows Him to protect He gives to His servants.

SPIRITS OF DEVINATION BELIEVE IN THE MOST HIGH GOD. (Acts 16:16-18)

This was an evil spirit of divination in the girl that allowed her to tell fortunes. This same *spirit* that revealed to her that these servants were the "ministers of the God, proving that this *spirit* knew there is a "Most High God" and he had God.

EVIL SPIRITS BELIEVE AND KNOW CHRIST. (Acts 19:15-16)

This "evil spirit" believed in both Jesus and the Apostle Paul.

DEMONS BELIEVE AND FEAR GOD (James 2:19)

It is surely true that the "demons believe" in God. The "wicked" who do not believe are *worse* than demons!

Chapter 5

THE DEVIL AND HIS DEMONS CONFESS GOD

The previous chapter demonstrated that Satan and his demons professed their faith in the Most High God and His Son, Jesus Christ. We will now look at Scripture that highlights their "confessions".

THE SERPENT CONFESSES GOD TO THE WOMAN. (Genesis 3:1; Genesis 3:4-5)

The serpent confessed God in these two verses by asking and telling Eve, "Did God really say...and God knows..." by admitting there is a God when he referred to Him twice in the way that he did.

SATAN'S CONFESSION. (Job 1:9-10)

In the Devil's statement, he confessed that there is a God and He protected Job on every side, making it impossible for Satan to try him out.

A LEGION OF DEMONS CONFESS JESUS AS SON OF GOD. (Luke 8:27-30; Matthew 8:28-32; Mark 5:1-15; Luke 8:28)

THE UNCLEAN SPIRIT MADE TWO CONFESSIONS. (Mark 1:23-24; Luke 4:33-34)

This unclean spirit confessed Christ two times. First, that He is "Jesus of Nazareth"; second that "He is the Holy One of God".

MANY DEVILS CONFESS JESUS. (Luke 4:41)

Jesus had his own "time table" as to when he wanted His disciples and the world to know who He was and his purpose. It was not yet time for Jesus to reveal this, and these devils so confessed Him that He had to force them not to speak. They knew He is the Christ and were not shy about telling it to others!

EVIL SPIRIT CONFESSES CHRIST AND PAUL. (Acts 19:12-16)

"Jesus I know and Paul I know, but who are you?" This evil spirit knew Jesus and Paul much better than he did this wicked, hypocritical chief priest, who, instead of being true to God himself, was practicing witchery upon the people.

Today there are millions who reject God and Jesus Christ. They deny that He exists and are enemies of Christianity. There are teachers in our public and private schools, professors in universities and other high places of learning that are robbing our sons and daughters of their faith in God, Christ, the Bible and the Church. Unless we raise our children in the "discipline and "instruction" of the Lord (Ephesians 6:4), we will continue to see our younger generation fall "prey" to Satan. This is exactly how he does his best work!

Chapter 6

ALL IN THE FAMILY

Scripture reveals there is a "Devil Family": a "Father Devil", a "Mother Devil", and many "Devil Children."

The Father Devil
ONE OF HIS NAMES IS "FATHER." (John 8:41-44)
Unrighteous people have no right to say, "Our Father, Who art in heaven". They have no heavenly father. They belong to the Devil Family, he is their father.

SATAN IS CALLED THE "PRINCE" OF DEMONS. (Matthew 9:34; Matthew 12:24; Mark 3:22)
He is not only the Prince of Demons, he is the "King of all Demons".

SATAN IS "CHIEF" OF DEMONS. (Luke 11:15)
Since he is called "Father Devil", Prince of Demons", and "Chief of Demons", this would certainly designate him as head of the "Devil Family".

HE IS CALLED "BEELZEBUL or BEELZEBUB". (Matthew 10:25; Matthew 12:24; Matthew 12:27; Mark 3:22; Luke 11:18-19)

"Beelzebub" or "Beelzebul" means the "Lord of dung", which reveals that he is the head of a rotten and disgusting family!

ANOTHER NAME FOR THE DEVIL IS "PRINCE OF THIS WORLD". (John 14:30)

Jesus recognized that the Devil is the "Prince of this world", the head of all worldliness, even the head of the "Devil Family".

HIS NAME IS THE "GOD OF THIS WORLD". (2 Corinthians 4:3-4)

Being the god of this world also qualifies him as the head of the "Devil Family". The Devil owns the "kingdoms" of this world, and he offered Christ all of them, if only he would bow down and worship him.

THE MOTHER DEVIL (Galatians 4:26)

The Bible speaks of the heavenly Jerusalem above us, the Mother of Christians, then it is only logical for that opposite place—hell—would be the mother of the wicked, including her children!

> Woe to you, scribes and Pharisees, hypocrites! For you travel around by sea and land to make one proselyte; and when he becomes one, you make him twice as much of a son of Gehenna *hell* as yourselves. (Matthew 23:15)

So the "Mother of Hell" does have children.

Satan's Children

We will see that he does have children, through Biblical proof. The Word of God gives us these answers, if we will only study this Inspired book. Let's see what it reveals about children of the Devil, and all of the Devil Family.

SEED OF THE SERPENT. (Genesis 3:15; Revelation 12:7-9)

Just as the woman has "seed", so does the Devil. Between his offspring—wicked angels and wicked people—there has always been an endless war on this earth.

These Scriptures all show that wicked angels belong to the Devil, that they are members of his family, and they are his children by adoption.

WEEDS ARE "CHILDREN OF THE WICKED ONE". (Matthew 13:38)

All "weeds", wicked people, are the Children of the Devil. They are part of the Devil Family.

THE APOSTLE PETER WAS CALLED SATAN. (Matthew 16:23; Mark 8:33)

When Peter spoke against God's plan for His Son, Jesus called him Satan.

JUDAS WAS OF THE DEVIL. (John 6:70-71; John 13:27; John 17:12; John 13:2)

When Judas betrayed Christ, he became a member of the "Devil Family". Today, the same is true of those now who would betray Christ by their unrighteous living.

ELYMAS THE SORCERER WAS A CHILD OF THE DEVIL. (Acts 13:8-11)

According to the Apostle Paul, Elymas was a "child of the Devil". This would include any other person that perverts the Scriptures, teaches false doctrines.

"CHILDREN OF DISOBEDIENCE". (Ephesians 5:6)

Those people who are disobedient all belong to the "Devil Family."

"THE MAN OF SIN" IS THE "SON OF DESTRUCTION". (2 Thessalonians 2:3)

Any "man of sin" is the "son of destruction". Sin makes any person a member of the "Devil Family".

HE THAT COMMITS SIN IS OF THE DEVIL. (1 John 3:8)

Sin makes anyone a member of the "Devil Family".

THE CHILDREN OF THE DEVIL. (1 John 3:10)

Unrighteousness or hating our brethren in the church will remove us from God's family and put us into the Devil's.

"YOU ARE OF YOUR FATHER THE DEVIL". (John 8:44)

All wicked people, if they pray should say, "Our father who art in hell". The Lord God is not their Father! Jesus called it like it is; the Devil is the father of the wicked.

POLITICAL ROME WAS A CHILD OF THE DEVIL. (Revelation 12:3; Revelation 12:9; Revelation 17:15; Revelation 13:1-7)

The book of Revelation gives a stark description of his horns and their symbol of power and kingdoms.

Listed below are the things that prove this was Political Rome:
- One head was wounded, showing it warred.
- "All the world wonder after the beast", showing it had world influence over nations.
- "Who is like the beast" shows he had more power than other people.
- "Who is like the beast" indicates that it was a warring power.
- "Power was given to him forty-two months (three and one-half years)" while Political Rome allied with Papal Rome. This time was known as the "Dark Ages".
- "And it was given to him to make war with the saints and to overcome them." This Political and Papal Rome literally did, causing the death of over seventy million Christians.
- "And power was given to every tribe, tongues and nations" means it was a political power, that it was a nation, and that it was WORLD POWER.

Since Jesus Christ, we have had but one such power, Political Rome.
- Since the beast is Political Rome, next Scripture shows he favors his father, the Devil.
- The Devil (and beast) has a red body. (Revelation 12:3 and 17:3) The Dragon or Devil (and beast) has seven heads. (Revelation 12:3; 13:1)

- The Dragon or Devil (and beast) has ten horns. (Revelation 12:3; 13:1) The Devil (and beast) has many crowns. (Revelation 12:3; 13:1)
- The Devil (and beast) wars against Christians. (Revelation 12:3-11; 13:7) The Devil (and beast) is a murderer. (John 8:44; and Revelation 13:7, 15.)
- The Devil is a liar and the beast is a liar and blasphemes God and His people. (John 8:44; Revelation 13:5-6)

As mentioned earlier, Revelation consists of visions of the Apostle John and focuses primarily on prophetic events written in Apocalyptic style.

If a son is the image of his father in these things, then there is no doubt of their relationship. We have found in these the "Son Devil", Political Rome, is the exact image of his father the "Father Devil", the Old Dragon himself. This portrays Political Rome as the Devil!

PAPAL ROME IS A GRANDCHILD OF THE DEVIL. (Revelation 13:11)

Political Rome is a child of this beast. In Chapter 13 of Revelation, an alliance is revealed between them. As mentioned above, Political Rome is a child of the Devil, and now this product, this child of Political Rome, has the "Voices of the Dragon", his grandfather's voice; thus, it is the grandchild of the Devil. It tries to conceal the relationship by appearing with only two horns, lamb like horns, pretending to be a "wolf in sheep's clothing." Since the beast has the "voice of the dragon", it cannot disguise itself. He belongs to the

"Dragon Family". These two beasts are Political and Papal Rome. The Bible again reveals that these two powers are children of the Devil. When we sin, we become children of Satan and become part of the "Devil Family"!

THE DEVIL'S FROG LIKE CHILDREN. (Revelation 16:13-14)

These are Devil spirits out of the mouth of the Dragon, described as the beast and false prophet. They too are children in the "Devil Family".

Chapter 7

MIRACLES OR MAGICIANS

Satan has wonderful power, and he furnishes his servants' power to an amazing degree. He deceives many, making them believe that his wonders and miracles were performed by the power of God. In the book of Exodus, we see Satan using his magicians to challenge God in performing miracles of the ten plagues to force Pharaoh to release God's people:

Turning the Nile River to blood.
Plague of the frogs
Plague of the Lice
Plague of the Flies
Pestilence, which killed Cattle and Sheep
Plague of Boils
Plague of Hail
Plague of Darkness
The Death of the Egyptian Firstborn and Beasts

Satan used Pharaoh's magicians to duplicate all but one of these plagues.

THOSE WHO WOULD WORK MIRACULOUS POWER TO DECEIVE RIGHTEOUS PEOPLE. (Matthew 24:24)

Many have tried to deceive real Christians by Satanic miracles. They are to know the truth and not be "carried about with every wind of doctrine."

SATAN'S SIGNS AND LYING WONDERS. (2 Thessalonians 2:8-9)

There appears to be real "wonders" and real "signs" but they are "lying wonders"! If we are not careful and knowledgeable of God's Word, we may be lead astray from the truth by them.

CAUSING FIRE TO COME DOWN FROM HEAVEN. (Revelation 13:11-14)

Satan performs some of his best "magic". Pulling down fire out of the sky is no small feat, but he managed to pull it off by trickery.

UNCLEAN SPIRITS WORKING MIRACLES. (Revelation 16:13-14)

These evil spirits heal the sick, pull down fire from the sky, and do many wonders to deceive all but God's people.

SORCERERS DECEIVE NATIONS. (Revelation 18:23)

Modern day sorcerers are known as fortune tellers. Religious deceit of this kind can cause a person to lose their soul to the Devil.

FALSE PROPHETS PERFORM MIRACLES. (Revelation 19:20)

God Himself calls them "real" miracles. He allows them to be accomplished by the power of the Devil and false prophets. This miracle causes one to be cast into the lake of fire!

SATAN MAKES SNAKES. (Exodus 7:8-12)

Satan's magicians of Egypt made snakes. God then let Aaron make a "king snake" by the power of God. It then swallowed all of the Devil made snakes. God showed the Devil that he was limited in his power.

SATAN TURNS THE NILE RIVER INTO BLOOD. (Exodus 7:19-20)

The magicians of Satan then made blood as easily as they had created snakes. Since the Devil himself first appeared to Eve as a snake, he knew how to make one.

THE DEVIL MATCHED AARON IN MAKING FROGS. (Exodus 8:5-7)

Satan was looking good and gaining confidence making snakes, blood and frogs, but he finally met his match!

THE DEVIL TRIED TO MAKE LICE BUT COULD NOT. (Exodus 8:16-19)

The Devil thought that he could match God's power anytime, anyplace, but quickly found out that he could not. He could match God with making snakes, blood, and frogs—BUT, HE COULD NOT MAKE LICE! Today, supposed miracle workers try to heal people and raise them from the dead. Why can't they? Because ONLY GOD IS ALL POWERFUL!

THE DEVIL'S MIRACLE WORKERS IN THE JUDGMENT. (Matthew 7:21-23; Matthew 15:14; Matthew 10:7-8)

The Bible clearly tells us how the "source of miracles" were identified, whether they be of God or the Devil.

Chapter 8

THE DEVIL IS A FAILURE

Powerful as he is, Satan is not always successful in what he attempts to do to man. Listed below are some of his worst failures, as well as his followers.

THE DEVIL'S SNAKES WERE SWALLOWED. (Exodus 7:10-12)
With this one of many failures, the Devil did not give up on his efforts then, or today.

HE COULD NOT MAKE LICE. (Exodus 8:17-19)
The magicians of the Devil admitted their defeat, saying "This is the finger of God", admitting that they were not using "God's Power", but Satan's. Failing to make lice was the only Egyptian plague of the ten that he could not match.

SATAN FAILED TO MAKE JOB CURSE GOD. (Job 1:13-19; 9:1-12)

Satan's goal was to make Job curse God, but he failed miserably, as follows:
- o He had the Sabeans carry away his livestock after killing his servants.
- o He brought down fire from heaven, burning up his sheep and servants.
- o He sent the Chaldeans to kill his servants and carried away his camels.
- o He sent a mighty wind that blew away his house, killing his children.

After all of this torture, Job remained faithful to God!

> Then Job arose, and tore his robe, and shaved his head, and fell down on the ground, and worshiped. He said, "Naked I came out of my mother's womb, and naked shall I return there. Yahweh gave, and Yahweh has taken away. Blessed be Yahweh's name." In all this, Job did not sin, nor charge God with wrongdoing. (Job 1:20-22)

God won a great victory in the life of one of His servants, and Satan suffered his greatest defeat! Job blessed the name of the Lord. Satan could not cause him to sin against God.

HE FAILED A SECOND TIME TO MAKE JOB CURSE GOD. (Job 2:4-9)

This time, Satan put forth his "best effort" to make Job curse God, again he failed!
- o "He afflicted Job with painful sores all over his body."
- o He also sent three men, Job's friends, accusing him of being unfaithful, giving that

  as the cause of his suffering.
- His wife told him to curse God and die,

> But he said to her, "You speak as one of the foolish women would speak. What? Shall we receive good at the hand of God, and shall we not receive evil?" In all this, Job didn't sin with his lips. (Job 2:10)

> No temptation has taken you except what is common to man. God is faithful, who will not allow you to be tempted above what you are able, but will with the temptation also make the way of escape, that you may be able to endure it. (1 Corinthians 10:13)

THE DEVIL ATTEMPTED TO KEEP AN ANGEL FROM GOING TO DANIEL AND BLESSING HIM. (Daniel 10:12-13, 20)

In Daniel 10:1-11, Daniel went on a fast to cleanse himself, pray and better understand the will of the Lord. After beginning the fast, God sent the angel Gabriel, as he generally visited Daniel. However, on the way to Daniel, this angel was intercepted by an evil spirit described as, the "Prince of the kingdom of Persia". This "evil being" fought with the Gabriel for twenty-one days and would not allow him to get to Daniel. Then, God sent a second angel, Michael, who fought with this "Prince of the kingdom of Persia", who lets the other angel go on to Daniel, receives his words and blesses him. Satan was determined that the angel should not get to Daniel with the blessing, but the angel, Michael, defeated the Devil.

HE FAILED TO GET CHRIST TO MAKE BREAD OUT OF STONES. (Matthew 4:1-4)

Jesus confirms his answer to Satan by quoting Deuteronomy 8:3. Satan cannot quote that Scripture; Jesus is not bowing to the temptation.

HE TRIES TO GET JESUS TO LEAP FROM THE TOP OF THE TEMPLE. (Matthew 4:5-6)

Did Jesus jump from the temple top? Jesus' answer:

> "Again, it is written, 'You shall not test the Lord, your God." (Matthew 4:7)

The Devil tried to quote Psalm 91:11-12 but failed. Once again, Satan is the loser!

HE TRIED TO GET CHRIST TO FALL DOWN AND WORSHIP HIM. (Matthew 4:8-9)

Did Jesus accept the Devil's offer this time? You already know the answer, absolutely not!

> Then Jesus said to him, "Get behind me, Satan! For it is written, 'You shall worship the Lord your God, and you shall serve him only.'" (Matthew 4:10)

Christ quoted from Deuteronomy 6:13 and 10:20. Each of the three times, Jesus won the victory by quoting the Scriptures. The Devil had no "come back", he was speechless. That will be the same "condition" of all the wicked on the day of judgment.

HE FAILS TO PREVAIL AGAINST THE CHURCH. (Matthew 16:18)

Every setback that the Devil has ever given to the

Church has proven to be an advantage for the Church. She always comes back with victory and more glory than ever. All the devils of hell cannot destroy the Church bought with the blood of Jesus Christ.

SATAN FAILS IN THE GREAT CHURCH WAR. (Revelation 12:7-9)

The Church is this "heaven", the great war between right and wrong. If this war took place in God's heaven, then it would prove that sin originated up there, along with death. Then, how is the Satan to be overcome and cast out of the "Church heaven?"

- "They triumphed over him by the blood of the Lamb". (Revelation 12:11)
- They do not have flesh and blood in God's heaven. (1 Corinthians 15:50)
- "And by the word of their testimony": they must do it by preaching the Word and testifying through it. (Revelation 12:11)
- "They did not love their lives so much as to shrink from death." (Revelation 12:11)
- People must die to get the Devil out of this "Church heaven", this is earthly heaven. Satan will utterly fail and have to move his seat to a place outside of the church, as now his seat is in the Church. (Revelation 2:13)

HE CANNOT DROWN THE CHURCH WOMAN. (Revelation 12:15)

People represent waters in the book of Revelation. Satan brought forth every possible follower he had against the Church Woman trying to drown her by using mass numbers of his followers. Did he succeed?

> The earth helped the woman, and the earth opened its mouth and swallowed up the river which the dragon spewed out of his mouth. (Revelation 12:16)

Instead of his great numbers of people flooding the Church out of existence, it speculates that they would fight their own numbers to the death instead, and all be taken down by the grave mouths of the earth. Their being "swallowed" by the earth represented the numbers being put into their graves.

THE DEVIL FAILS IN THE GOG-MAGOG WAR. (Revelation 20:7-9)

In the Apostle John's vision in Revelation, Satan will be loosed and deceive wicked nations into warring against the "Camp of the Saints" at the close of the thousand years or millennium. The people of God will be separated during this time. Who will succeed? The Devil and all his followers fail miserably. God and all of His people will be triumphant and spend eternity in "God's heaven", praising Him!

HIS LAST FAILURE, BEING CONSUMED IN THE LAKE OF FIRE. (Revelation 20:10)

Satan's journey began in the Garden of Eden and will end when he and ALL of his followers are cast into the lake of fire and brimstone. He has caused much trouble to this day and will continue until he lands into his eternal imprisonment where he will suffer for all eternity the agonies that he wanted ALL mankind to suffer. We know that God is MOST HIGH, Christ is ALL and ALL, victorious over Satan. We as Christians are NOT fighting a losing battle, as long as we keep our faith and trust in God to the end of our journey home to those mansions prepared for us by Jesus Christ.

Chapter 9

SATAN AND DEMONS OBEY GOD AND CHRIST

Although Satan is the most powerful evil spiritual being, he is, and has always been, under the subjection of God. God limits his power for His purpose on this earth. Satan's demons as well are subject to God's will and complete control. Presented now are examples of his and their obedience unto God.

THE DEVIL OBEYED GOD BY NOT TOUCHING JOB PHYSICALLY. (Job 1:12-22)

God gave Satan the power to destroy everything Job had. However, he was not to touch Job physically. These verses reveal that Satan never interfered with Job physically, never touched his body; he obeyed God in this matter.

SATAN OBEYED GOD IN SAVING JOB'S LIFE. (Job

2:6; 42:16-17)

Satan obeyed as commanded. God then gave him the power to touch Job's flesh this time, to do anything to him but kill him. Satan did put sores all over his body but did not kill him!

HE LEFT JESUS AS HE WAS COMMANDED. (Matthew 4:10-11)

The Devil left Christ and he was immediately replaced by angels attending Christ.

EVIL SPIRITS EVEN OBEYED HIS WORD. (Matthew 8:16)

Christ commanded the spirits to leave and they obeyed his command.

A MUTE DEVIL OBEYED. (Matthew 9:33)

This devil left the man at Christ's command.

THE DEMON OBEYED JESUS BY LEAVING A CHILD. (Matthew 17:18)

The child was acting "crazy" and immediately left his body when commanded by Jesus.

UNCLEAN SPIRITS OBEYED CHRIST. (Mark 1:27; Luke 4:36)

Plainly documented, unclean spirits obeyed Him.

DEVILS OBEYED CHRIST BY REMAINING SILENT. (Mark 1:34)

Many in today's world need to "keep silent"!

DEVILS OBEYED CHRIST IN THE SYNAGOGUES. (Mark 1:39)

Some demons in that day possessed people who attended the synagogues. At Christ's command, they left the synagogues.

DEMONS WERE CALLED TO OBEY THE APOSTLES. (Mark 6:13)

The apostles had the power to command demons to leave people, and they did.

THERE WAS A DEMON THAT LEFT A GIRL AT CHRIST'S COMMAND. (Mark 7:29-30)

On one occasion, Jesus commanded a devil to go out of a girl from a distance, and immediately the demon obeyed.

A NONBELIEVER WAS CASTING OUT DEMONS THROUGH CHRIST'S POWER. (Mark 9:38)

Some besides Jesus and the apostles had the power to cast out demons.

SEVEN UNCLEAN SPIRITS OBEYED CHRIST AT ONCE. (Luke 8:2; Mark 16:9)

No matter how many demons possessed a person, at Jesus' command they were all cast out immediately.

A LEGION OF DEVILS OBEYED CHRIST. (Luke 8:29-31)

There were enough demons in that man to enter two thousand hogs and run them into the sea. Christ ordered them out and they left immediately.

A DEVIL TORMENTED THE BOY, BUT OBEYED CHRIST. (Luke 9:42)

This was a vicious impure spirit that immediately obeyed Jesus to come out of the boy.

DEMONS OBEYED THE SEVENTY. (Luke 10:17)

The Seventy had the power of Christ, and even the devils obeyed them. (See Chapter 2.)

A DEVIL OBEYED BY LEAVING A MUTE MAN. (Luke 11:14)

By the command of Christ, devils left this man immediately.

PAUL COMMANDED A SPIRIT OF DEVINATION TO OBEY HIM. (Acts 16:16-18)

Did the spirit come out of the woman at Paul's command? Immediately.

Many people today fail to obey the Gospel of Christ for their Salvation. But the day will come when they wish they had!

EVIL SPIRITS OBEYED PAUL FROM AFAR. (Acts 19:11-12)

Like Jesus, Paul did not have to be present for demons to obey him. Even garments that he had touched, that were sent to other places, when they touched the demon-possessed person, those evil spirits obeyed and left immediately!

All the examples of demons leaving people were very much against their will. They were driven out by the power of God. Serving God today through "fear of force" is not God's plan. He certainly expects and deserves our total respect. His desire is that we love him with all of our heart, soul, and mind and serve him willfully. We should serve the true and living God because it is right and because we love him and want to praise and worship him for eternity!

Chapter 10

THE MASTER COUNTERFEITER

According to the dictionary, "counterfeit" means to exactly imitate something valuable or important with the intention to deceive or defraud. This crime is generally committed for a twenty-dollar bill or higher domination in US currency. The Federal Reserve spends millions of dollars on paper and equipment, plus many man hours to try and stay ahead of these professional counterfeiters! We see the same efforts for high-end products such as watches, handbags, and many expensive articles of clothing that are popular with the general public.

Imagine what it costs when God's Word, and especially the Plan of Salvation, are counterfeited. The greatest of all cost: the *loss of a person's soul!* This happens worldwide by those who would teach other than the Gospel of Christ to those with "itching ears"! (2 Timothy 4:3.) Who has always been responsible for teaching error? The "Master Counterfeiter", the Devil himself!

SATAN COUNTERFEITS CHRIST. (John 8:12; 2 Corinthians 11:14)

Satan does his best to convince mankind that he is the Light of the World, as is Christ.

The Devil knows that his only hope of fooling the world is to imitate Christ. Being a counterfeit is his deception to win over as many souls as possible. Knowledge of the Word of God clearly identifies the difference in the two "lights". We know that Christ is the TRUE LIGHT!

THE DEVIL COUNTERFEITS THE APOSTLES. (2 Corinthians 11:13; Revelation 2:2)

In 2 Corinthians 11:13, Paul tells us that we have counterfeit apostles. Revelation 2:2 tells us there were counterfeit apostles in the Ephesian Church who were proven to be liars. Many counterfeit apostles made their appearance during and since the days of Paul and John. The original apostles were truly the New Testament disciples of Christ.

HE COUNTERFEITS MINISTERS. (2 Corinthians 11:15)

Since the beginning of time, there has always been and always will be "false preachers and teachers" who pervert "God's Word". The Devil's servants are "counterfeit ministers of righteousness."

HE COUNTERFEITS THE SCRIPTURES. (Corinthians 2:17)

"Peddling the Word of God for profit" means

counterfeiting, perverting and misusing it.

Paul warns us again:

> But we have renounced the hidden things of shame, not walking in craftiness, nor handling the word of God deceitfully; but by the manifestation of the truth commending ourselves to every man's conscience in the sight of God. (2 Corinthians 4:2)

These Scriptures show that the Devil leads preachers to handle the Word of God deceitfully. This is one way to "sell the souls of men." Mishandling the Word of God is counterfeiting it!

SATAN COUNTERFEITS THE PLAN OF SALVATION. (Acts 15:1, 24)

Did these ministers come from the Jerusalem Church, from God? No. These were counterfeit ministers and false teachers. Their preaching divided the churches, causing havoc among those new congregations.

Counterfeiting God's Plan of Salvation may grieve Him more than any other distortion of the Gospel! (See Chapter 19)

THE DEVIL COUNTERFEITS DOCTRINE. (Matthew 15:9; Mark 7:7 Romans 16:17; 1 Corinthians 14:26; Ephesians 4:14; 1 Timothy 1:10; Hebrews 13:9)

From the beginning of the Church until today, there are counterfeit ministers teaching "contrary doctrines", "doctrines of men".

The Corinthian and Ephesian churches both struggled with false doctrine. Sexual wickedness is contrary to "sound doctrine". (1 Timothy 1:10) Those ministers who condone such are counterfeiters. It is all around us today!

The Devil's counterfeit doctrines have always been taught in Paul's day until today.

HE COUNTERFEITS THE CUP OF THE LORD AND TABLE OF THE LORD. (1 Corinthians 10:21)

This Scripture shows that in Paul's day, counterfeit teachers had even perverted the "cup of the Lord." What a terrible thing to fall away so far from God to take in vain the "memorial supper" of Christ's shed blood on the cross! The Bible specifically instructs us how often to drink of the "cup of the Lord", for what purpose, and in what manner. Otherwise it becomes counterfeit and becomes the "cup of devils".

Again, the Bible gives us specific instructions on partaking of the memorial "Lord's Supper", *eating of the bread* (representing Christ's broken body on the cross) and *drinking of the cup* (representing His shed blood on the cross in our stead). To partake of these emblems in an unworthy manner is a counterfeited memorial to Christ's sacrifice for our sins.

SATAN COUNTERFEITS THE CHURCH. (Matthew 16:18)

The Church, established by Christ in 33 AD, is the "One True Church". *all others* since that time are counterfeit!

The Devil has counterfeited everything essential to salvation. "God's True Plan of Salvation" is explained in Chapter 19.

Chapter 11

NINE HEAVENS

There is an expression: "I am in seventh heaven!" This phrase generally refers to a condition of extreme joy. When you ask a child where heaven is, he or she will generally point upward. We are taught that "heaven" is above and is the home of God. Did you know that Scripture teaches there are actually *nine* different heavens?

The first, or *"Beginning Heaven"* is revealed in Genesis 1:1:

> In the beginning, God created the *heavens* and the earth.

Philippians 3:20 talks about *"Christ's Home Heaven"*:

> For our citizenship is in *heaven*, from where we also wait for a Savior, the Lord Jesus Christ.

The next seven heavens found in Scripture refer to those that are on or near the earth.

Genesis 1:6-8 talks about the *"Firmament Heaven"*:

> And God said, Let there be a *firmament* in the midst of the waters, and let it divide the waters from the waters. And God made the *firmament*, and divided the waters which were under the *firmament* from the waters which were above the *firmament*: and it was so. And God called the *firmament* Heaven.

We learn about the *"Star Heaven"* and *"Cloud Heaven"* in Matthew 24:29-30:

> Immediately after the tribulation of those days shall the sun be darkened, and the moon shall not give her light, and the *stars* shall fall from *heaven*, and the powers of the heavens shall be shaken: And then shall appear the sign of the Son of man in heaven: and then shall all the tribes of the earth mourn, and they shall see the Son of man coming in the *clouds* of *heaven* with power and great glory.

The "Dew Heaven" is recorded in Daniel 4:15:

> Nevertheless leave the stump of his roots in the earth, even with a band of iron and brass, in the tender grass of the field; and let it be wet with the *dew* of *heaven*, and let his portion be with the beasts in the grass of the earth. Therefore the heaven over you is stayed from dew, and the earth is stayed from her fruit.

Haggai 1:10 records a second referral to the dew heaven, which is all over the earth, not God's heavenly home.

Genesis 1:20 tells of the *"Fowl Heaven"*:

> And God said, Let the waters bring forth abundantly the moving creature that hath life,

and *fowl* that may fly above the earth in the open *firmament* of *heaven*.

All kinds of birds are flying in the *Fowl Heaven* below on the earth.

Next, we learn of the *Rain Heaven*. This heaven is just above us and supplies rain on the earth.

> In the six hundredth year of Noah's life, in the second month, on the seventeenth day of the month, on the same day all the fountains of the great deep were burst open, and the sky's windows were opened. It rained on the earth forty days and forty nights. (Genesis 7:11-12)

> "And then the Lord's wrath be kindled against you, and he shut up the *heaven*, that there be no rain, and that the land yield not her fruit; and lest ye perish quickly from off the good land which the Lord giveth you." (Deuteronomy 11:17)

The Lord was angered and caused no rain to fall upon the earth.

> "The Lord shall open unto thee his good treasure, the *heaven* to give the rain unto thy land in his season, and to bless all the work of thine hand: and thou shalt lend unto many nations, and thou shalt not borrow." (Deuteronomy 28:12)

God richly pours out rain upon the earth. It falls on both the "just" and the "unjust" (Matthew 5:45).

> Who covers the *heaven* with clouds, who prepares rain for the earth, who makes grass to grow upon the mountains. (Psalm 147:8)

> I saw in the night visions, and, behold, one like the Son of man came with the clouds of *heaven*, and came to the Ancient of days, and they

brought him near before him. (Daniel 7:13)

The clouds in which Daniel saw Jesus coming from this heaven is the sky above us that we see with our own eyes.

James 5:18 plainly tells us that the rain coming from this "heaven" is just above us on the earth.

Scripture mentions the *Star Heaven* in Matthew 24:29. For "stars to fall from heaven" then this heaven must be located in the outer most parts of the universe, far above the earth, and the dew, rain and cloud heavens.

> But immediately after the oppression of those days, the sun will be darkened, the moon will not give its light, the stars will fall from the sky, and the powers of the *heavens* will be shaken.

And last, but certainly not least, *Christians' Earthly Home Heaven* is mentioned in Ephesians 1:3:

> Blessed be the God and Father of our Lord Jesus Christ, who hath blessed us with all spiritual blessings in *heavenly places* in Christ.

So, here we have the nine heavens revealed in Scripture:

Christ's Home Heaven (Philippians 3:20)
Beginning Heaven (Genesis 1:1)
(The seven listed below are here or in sight of the earth.)
Firmament Heaven (Genesis 1:6-8)
Cloud Heaven (Matthew 24:30)
Rain Heaven (Genesis 7:11-12)
Dew Heaven (Daniel 4:15)
Fowl Heaven (Genesis 1:20)
Star Heaven (Matthew 24:29)
Christians' Earthly Home heaven (Ephesians 1:3)

The seven heavens are so closely related that it is difficult to tell where one ends and the other begins. The *Christians' Earthly Home Heaven* is where we live and walk daily by the side of our Lord and Savior, Jesus Christ, on this earth, which makes it far different from the other six *"lower heavens"*. Remember, this is the heaven where Satan has *always resided* and *wars with humanity*. But, on that judgment day, Satan, his angels, and all those who are outside of Christ, His Church, shall be cast down to hell, the lake of fire burning with brimstone where they shall remain in eternal torment!

Chapter 12

THE SNAKE

Since the beginning of time, the "Snake" has been the nemesis of mankind. This slimy serpent first appeared and grabbed the attention of Adam, and especially Eve, in the Garden of Eden. Yes, this particular snake is "the Devil" himself! Until we understand him and his mission on this earth, we cannot fully understand God and His great purpose for man and that Heaven up yonder.

THE TALKING SERPENT. (Genesis 3:1, 4-5; Revelation 12:9; Revelation 20:2)

We quickly learn what this snake is called. The "snake" is the Devil and Satan, the one that deceives the whole world. God's Word first calls the Devil a Serpent because of the "poison" that he injects into humanity. This was no ordinary snake that entered the Garden of Eden, but the Devil himself! The Devil is a "talker", a master communicator. He and all of his followers are "masters of deceit".

THE SERPENT'S TONGUE BURNS WITH THE FIRE OF HELL. (James 3:6)

THE CRAWLING SERPENT. (Genesis 3:14-15)

The Devil is cursed to "crawl through life", to be one of the lowest creatures on earth. His followers also receive that "punishment", although they may not realize it now. Only the good are "upright", they stand up and walk by the grace of God. Sinners are wounded in their heels.

On the other hand, Christians "walk by faith" (2 Corinthians 5:7). If we choose to follow Satan, we will have "foot trouble and even have to crawl", but we can avoid this problem if we "walk by faith" in Jesus Christ.

THE DIRT-EATING SERPENT. (Genesis 3:14; Isaiah 65:25; Psalm 78:25; John 6:53-58)

Here Jesus is referring to regularly partaking of the "Lord's Supper" to always remember Christ's death, burial, and resurrection. He does refer to the good spiritual food having been sent from God's Heaven. Sinners know nothing about that "bread which is given by God". They are of the earth, and don't know about the good gifts that come from above.

> "Every good and perfect gift is from above, coming down from the Father of the heavenly lights, who does not change like shifting shadows." (James 1:17)

Sinners never feast on these blessings, but all that they eat grows out of the "dirt".

Until one hears the Word of God, believes, repents, confesses Jesus as the Son of God, and is baptized into Christ can they taste and continually eat of the "Fruits of God."

> You can't drink both the cup of the Lord and the cup of demons. You can't partake both of the table of the Lord, and of the table of demons. (1 Corinthians 10:21)

Chapter 13

BEST MAN

When man stood upright, sinless before God in the Garden of Eden, he was not yet to be a finished product. He was not through "making man". God had just made worlds, stars and suns as finished products. Unlike those creations, God knew that man was capable of everlasting growth and through future time He needed to give man help on his growth and development. It would surely be a sad day if man were to reach the end of all growing, all improvement and he should be informed that he could not become any sweeter, that he could not become any better, that he could not attain any more knowledge and that he could climb no higher. The heaven we have in this world is knowing, growing and doing worthwhile things, which is God's plan for His people.

> God said, "Let us make man in our image, after our likeness: and let them have dominion over the fish of the sea, and over the birds of the sky,

and over the livestock, and over all the earth, and over every creeping thing that creeps on the earth." (Genesis 1:26)

The question now comes: Who was God talking to when He said, "Let Us make man, in Our own image?" He was speaking to ALL things He had created, every world, every sun and every star in the universe, every devil, every angel and every Divine Being to be found anywhere in God's Almighty vast domain! Most importantly, He was speaking to *Christ* and *The Holy Spirit* as well.

God has set in motion His eternal task. The time will never come when God will say to man, "I have done all that is possible toward your growth and development on this earth." In the beginning when God made the first man, and he stood up in the very image of God, having not known of sin at all, that man was a "perfect product" at that point in time. He was sinless in every way! Jesus never sinned, but He was made perfect in suffering.

> "For it became Him, for whom are all things, and through whom are all things, in bringing many children to glory, to make the author of their salvation perfect through sufferings." (Hebrews 2:10)

A newborn baby is sinless, but the body, soul and spirit are not perfect. All must be trained and schooled into perfection. Since Adam was the "image" of God, he was the very best at the time, but He set out to make man in His likeness, meaning to be "like" God in every way.

It was God's greatest and eternal purpose to make man to become the greatest creature that the Godhead could make, using every created thing, every angel, and every devil as assistants. God will never cease to work on the development of His man. How He will produce the ultimate of mankind is one of the most intriguing things in the world.

Man's Ten Creators

GOD CREATED MAN. (Genesis 1:26; Romans 11:36)
This evolution theory is readily taught throughout our public schools, colleges and universities. Due to "political correctness" many Christians tend to shy away from "standing for the truth". God's Creation is *fact*, not fiction. It is way past time that we should stand strong on this matter. We WILL be held accountable!

CHRIST, MAN'S CREATOR. (John 1:3; Ephesians 3:17; John 17:9)

THE HOLY SPIRIT, MAN'S CREATORS. (Galatians 3:14; 2 Peter 1:21; Galatians 5:22-23
Since the Holy Spirit too is part of the "Trinity" *God, Son* and *Holy Spirit*, He was also included in the statement by God, "Let US make man". The Holy Spirit continues to this day to make man better. Apostle Paul speaks on this matter.
The "nine fruits" listed in Galatians 5:22-23 contribute to making the "greatest man" that the Trinity can make.

ANGELS ARE MAN'S CREATORS. (Psalm 34:7; Hebrews 1:14)
Here we also see angels playing a leading role in

man's development and growth.
- o Angels saved Elisha's life. (2 Kings 6:13-23)
- o Angels fought for Daniel and prevailed. (Daniel 10:1-20)
- o Christ was ministered to by angels after His battle with the Devil. (Matthew 4:11)
- o Angels gave comfort and strength to Christ in Gethsemane during his mental struggle with His upcoming crucifixion. (Luke 22:43)

THE BIBLE, MAN'S CREATOR. (2 Timothy 3:16-17)

The Bible helps to perfect man through furnishing him and encouraging him to do good works. God's Word, the Bible, is a lamp to man's feet directing him home to God. The Word reveals to us Jesus Christ, who is a model to each one of us, and how to walk in His ways.

THE CHURCH, MAN'S CREATOR. (Acts 2:47; John 10:9; Colossians 1:18)

This Scripture states that the church is the Body of Christ. We must be members of his Body, the Church, in order to partake of His Divine nature. We must grow into His likeness in order to become a citizen in his eternal home, God's heaven. Thus the Church contributes greatly to making us better human beings, created in Their (God, Christ and the Holy Spirit's) image.

INANIMATE THINGS MAN'S CREATORS. (2 Corinthians 4:15)

All God's creation is for our sake. We are too finite to even realize such things. But from this Scripture, Paul certainly realized it. On that day when we sit at the feet of the great Teacher—Jesus, He will make it all plain to us and show us the contribution that each thing made toward our Spiritual development, our Spiritual growth.

OTHER PEOPLE PART OF MAN'S CREATORS. (Romans 14:7; Hebrews 10:25)

There are some who try to live and die unto themselves. Some became the corrupt of all people as a result. It is essential that we, as a Christian Body, come together, supporting and encouraging each other to the betterment of our human and Spiritual growth.

THE DEVIL, ONE OF MAN'S CREATORS. (2 Corinthians 12:7)

It sounds absurd, but there is no doubt that Satan here is being used as a "blessing to man." Paul had received so many revelations from God that he was about to become "puffed up", but God prevented that by sending the messenger of Satan to torment him.

MAN IS RESPONSIBLE FOR ASSISTING IN HIS OWN CREATION. (Philippians 2:12)

While the other nine Creators have made their contributions toward making the greatest possible creature out of man, it would be a failure if man himself falls down on the job for improving upon his own development.

We have the choice to build a house of straw that will perish under the first fiery test or build upon the solid foundation of the Rock of Ages and withstand all the storms of life. "There were two men standing behind bars; one saw mud, the other saw stars." Our viewpoint depends on how we look at our purpose in life and our willingness to pay a higher price to climb to the mountain top!

With all ten Creators working continuously on our lives, making the best possible contributions, there can be no reason why we should not develop into the greatest creation, which is God's eternal plan for all of us.

Chapter 14

BEST HEAVEN

God never intended this world to be our eternal home. We are just traveling through, as the old hymn goes.

> "For we don't have here an enduring city, but we seek that which is to come." (Hebrews 13:14)

Abraham knew there was a better place than this old world.

> "For he looked for the city which has the foundations, whose builder and maker is God." (Hebrews 11:10)

Jesus offers comforting words for us, since this is not our final home.

> "Don't let your heart be troubled. Believe in God. Believe also in me. In my Father's house are many homes. If it weren't so, I would have told you. I am going to prepare a place for you. If I go and prepare a place for you, I will come again, and will receive you to myself; that where I am, you may be there also." (John 14:1-3)

God is a "star breather" and spoke into existence this world in which we are "temporary residents." It is a beautiful place, but we cannot even imagine the beauty and majesty of that "place" with "many mansions" where Christ has gone to prepare for the "saved." There is no description, known to man, that can furnish even a name for this eternal home of the soul, so Jesus just called it a "place", and in the land of the sky.

Just a clarification about that "place" which Jesus has gone to "prepare" for His own. Many think that it will be located down here on this earth, but this earth had been already been created when Jesus said He was "going" (not remaining here) to prepare a place. In Ephesians 4:10, Paul told us where Jesus was going when he left this earth to prepare a place:

> "He who descended is the one who also ascended far above *all the heavens,* that he might fill all things."

In the verse just given, God began to fill His creation with countless worlds and heavens. He would reserve the "grand" spot in the universe for Jesus to ascend after purchasing with his blood, human souls, and build a "Heavenly place" that only God could produce. Heavens, even all the heavens will pale away into everlasting insignificance compared with this place Jesus is preparing for us. Will all these present heavens pass away, and let this greatest of all places, take their place? Paul answers this question for us in Hebrews 1:10-11:

> And, 'You, Lord, in the beginning, laid the

> foundation of the earth. The heavens are the works of your hands. They will perish, but you continue.'

All of heavens that God ever made in the beginning will not even begin to compare to the place for man's new home, his haven of rest, his city of gold.

Since God is making for us the greatest home in glory that the Father, Son, Holy Spirit and angels combined can make, just think how much man must be refined and glorified before he could feel worthy to live in his eternal home. No wonder that God is taking such a long time to give man his training and using so many agents to accomplish this magnificent work. We are seeing that God is using the Devil to assist in making man to become the "best man" that he can be. God allows Satan to try us all the days of our lives. These trials will strengthen us to finally appreciate the beauty and wonderment of that place Jesus is preparing for us.

Then we can really realize what Paul meant in 2 Corinthians 4:16-17, when he said,

> Therefore we don't faint, but though our outward man is decaying, yet our inward man is renewed day by day. For our light affliction, which is for the moment, works for us more and more exceedingly as eternal weight of glory.

These sufferings are from the Devil, just as Job's were, and since they do add exceeding glory to us in that eternal home, we have to conclude that the Devil himself is being used by God in building the "best man" he can be, and the "best heaven" that can be made.

Chapter 15

MAN CAN BE BLESSED BY SATAN

Satan is the master tempter. As a result, he was able to reveal the perfection of Christ, as well as the best in other great men of the Bible. We can say the Devil blessed them by his temptations and sufferings.

KING DAVID WAS BLESSED BY THE DEVIL. (Psalm 119:67, 71)

Before David was afflicted, he went astray, even though God said of David that "He was a man after God's heart." David testified that it was good for him to be afflicted, that it caused him to learn and appreciate God's laws. We have to study the Word of God continually to appreciate our afflictions, losses, heartaches, disappointments and the Devil who causes all of these things.

APOSTLE PAUL WAS BLESSED BY SATAN. (2 Corinthians 12:7-10)

Paul prayed to God to take his "thorn in my flesh" away, but God let it remain. It is interesting that the Bible never identifies this thorn in the flesh. Listed below are the different blessings that came to Paul from the messenger of Satan—this "thorn":

- It humbled Paul throughout his life so that God could continue to use him for His purpose.
- Paul was given the full grace of God; he needed sympathy and help. He had a much greater appreciation of God and His purpose for him.
- God's strength covered Paul's weakness, allowing him to do God's bidding.
- Even though he suffered, Paul always gave God the glory and thanks for his infirmities.
- Since Paul had been the enemy of Christ, it caused the "power of Christ" to give him rest, comfort, and confidence like no other.
- Paul appreciated the cross of Christ by him too taking on the reproaches and sufferings of Christ during his life.
- It caused him to be happy in whatever situation that he found himself in at any time.
- Like Christ, he took pleasure in persecutions, which were many, for in his first defense he said he stood alone. (2 Timothy 4:26)
- He trusted God and took pleasure in getting into confrontations and struggles, knowing that God would show the way out.

- God always made him strong when he had been weak. (2 Corinthians 12:10)

WICKED CHURCH MEMBERS CORRECTED AND BLESSED BY THE DEVIL. (1 Corinthians 5:1-5)

The wicked man in these verses was a far worse fornicator because he sinned with his own father's wife. In order to reform this man from this serious sin, Paul advised the church to withdraw fellowship from him and turn him over to the Devil. By doing so, this would reform the man, save his spirit and soul. The Devil would actually bless this man by causing him great suffering!

1 Timothy 1:19-20 reveals a similar situation:

> Holding faith and a good conscience; which some having thrust away made a shipwreck concerning the faith; of whom is Hymenaeus and Alexander; whom I delivered to Satan, that they might be taught not to blaspheme.

These two men lost their faith, by making "shipwreck" of their Christian lives. Again, Satan was used to punish them, to turn them away from their blasphemy and sinful living. The Devil was used in both cases to reform those wicked church members. It may be that Satan is used by God from time to time to bring us back to our faithfulness to Him.

ALL CHURCH MEMBERS ARE BLESSED BY THE DEVIL. (2 Corinthians 4:8-12, 15-17)

Things in these verses that Christians suffer for:
- They are troubled from everywhere.
- They are harassed.

- They are confused.
- They are discouraged.
- They strive to imitate the dying of Christ.
- They are slaughtered for Christ's sake.
- Death cleanses in them. Every child of God must bear his crosses as a Christian for Christ and these are the blessings that following.
- They are not troubled.
- They never give up.
- They never feel rejected—the Lord never leaves them alone.
- They are never annihilated—they are always victorious.
- Happily, they commemorate the crucifixion of Christ in their lives.
- They joyfully suffer for Jesus' sake and are blessed by it.

Note the expression used in 2 Corinthians 4:15: "All things are for your sakes". Satan has been used in some manner for the blessing of man. God has used him to punish the human race for correction and to bring the disobedient back to Him.

> Before I was afflicted, I went astray; but now I observe your word. (Psalm 119:67)

All our earthly trials and struggles work for Christians making us ever stronger in our battle with Satan.

In James 1:2-4, we are told,

> "Count it all joy, my brothers, when you fall into various temptations, knowing that the testing of your faith produces endurance. Let endurance have its perfect work, that you may be perfect and complete, lacking in nothing."

This is God's way of strengthening us in this battle with the evil one. The Devil is used for our benefit and when we fully understand it, we can appreciate God more than ever before. Revelation 3:10 makes it very plain:

> "Because you kept my command to endure, I also will keep you from the hour of testing, which is to come on the whole world, to test those who dwell on the earth."

Abraham passed God's test by requiring that he offer his son, Isaac as a sacrifice. But Abraham more than met the challenge, coming out far greater and much happier than before. God tries us all, as it is most necessary for our good. We would never know our own weaknesses or strengths, without these afflictions and burdens in our lives.

Peter (in 1 Peter 4:12-13) speaks to our hearts on this subject:

> Beloved, don't be astonished at the fiery trial which has come upon you, to test you, as though a strange thing happened to you. But because you are partakers of Christ's sufferings, rejoice; that at the revelation of his glory you also may rejoice with exceeding joy.

Peter tells us that we are to have "fiery ordeals" to grow as Christians to be ready when Jesus comes in his glory. In 1 Peter 5:10, he speaks again:

> But may the God of all grace, who called you to his eternal glory by Christ Jesus, after you have suffered a little while, perfect, establish, strengthen, and settle you.

This is a most comforting verse when you consider the expression, "after you have suffered a little while." We suffer and die daily for the cause of Christ. The reward? An eternal home with God!

How we benefit from this "suffering":
- o We are made perfect in Christ.
- o He puts us on solid ground, both feet and on a solid rock.
- o He strengthens by overcoming temptations.
- o He stabilizes our faith.

In Hebrews 12:10-11, the Apostle Paul tells us:

> For they indeed, for a few days, punished us as seemed good to them; but he for our profit, that we may be partakers of his holiness. All chastening seems for the present to be not joyous but grievous; yet afterward it yields the peaceful fruit of righteousness to those who have been exercised thereby.

The theme of this chapter is that God uses Satan to discipline His people, as we have learned before.

> "And he will sit as a refiner and purifier of silver, and he will purify the sons of Levi, and refine them as gold and silver; and they shall offer to Yahweh offerings in righteousness." (Malachi 3:3)

When we fully understand this verse, we can realize this is one of the most beautiful verses in the Bible. The refiner was perfect in his "process" until the final product was perfect! So it is with us. Our lives are in a great crucible where Christ has placed us. He watches with close vigilance while Satan makes the fire hotter and hotter. The "fiery trial" is on, but as soon as Jesus sees Himself mirrored in our lives, He cools as we stand the test for Him.

We must be tested by the "heat of the Devil"

throughout our lives, to pass that final test, an eternal home in God's heaven.

JESUS WAS BLESSED BY SATAN. (Matthew 4:1-11)
The Devil tests the weak points in all of us. He tested Jesus in every way and found none. Jesus showed humanity His strength.

Jesus was tempted in all points (Hebrews 4:15) and the Devil served only to "perfect Him" (Hebrews 2:10). While in the Garden of Gethsemane, Jesus suffered every heartache; His sweat was drops of blood. These were his final temptations in the world by Satan. He even asked God, His Father, to take away His going to His death on the cross. But He knew this was His Father's Will, so He died for us. He was on His cross for nine hours to bring all of His suffering to a triumphant climax with the most wonderful PERFECTION that the world would ever see! And yes, Satan himself was a part of this and made his contribution to the perfection of our sinless Lord and Savior, Jesus Christ. Jesus reached perfection—His through suffering.

Satan had tried Jesus in every possible way, thus the world would see the strength of Christ in all His glory. He would become the greatest example of all time, under all circumstances. Satan tested Jesus throughout his short life, with us on this earth, but found no weaknesses! He withstood all of the "fiery darts" of the Devil. Yes, Satan blessed Jesus, because He overcame him in every battle. Satan blesses us today when we do as Paul did when he said: "I can do all things through Christ, who strengthens me."

Chapter 16

THE DEVIL MADE ME DO IT

Some of you are old enough to remember the television comedian, Flip Wilson, who was popular in the early 1970s. He created the line, "The Devil made me do it!" in his comedy routine. During a skit, when his character, Geraldine, would do something wrong, then asked why she did it, he would use this line.

When we think, say, or do something wrong, does the Devil make us do it? Does he make us commit any sin? Absolutely not! Then, if he doesn't, who does? *We* do, he only serves to tempt us. We either chose to sin or not.

> "No temptation has taken you except what is common to man. God is faithful, who will not allow you to be tempted above what you are able, but will with the temptation also make the way of escape, that you may be able to endure it." (1 Corinthians 10:13)

From the beginning, God gave man "Free Will". Man can choose Right or Wrong, Good or Evil! Because God knows the nature of man, he also provided in his Eternal Plan, a Savior, His Son Jesus Christ.

WE HAVE TWO CHOICES—LIFE (Genesis 2:9; Deuteronomy 30:15; Deuteronomy 30:19; Jeremiah 21:8; John 14:6) OR DEATH. (Romans 6:23)

OUR FREE WILL ALLOWS US TO CHOOSE EITHER LIFE OR DEATH. (Genesis 2:16-17; Deuteronomy 30:19; Joshua 24:15; 1 Kings 18:21; Matthew 11:28; Matthew 23:37; John 5:40; Acts 17:30; 2 Peter 3:9; Revelation 22:17)

God allowed Adam and Eve to make a choice: Eat or not eat from the "forbidden tree" in the garden.

Deuteronomy 30:19 compares Israel to Adam and Eve. Likewise, they had the same choice, life or death.

Israel was "not forced" by God to serve Him. He did encourage them to do so by keeping His commands, as it was certainly good for them. They could make a choice to serve other gods, as it was left entirely up to them. However, when they made that choice, the outcome was not good! You would think that Israel would learn their lesson after so many times suffering the consequences.

In 1 Kings 18:21 we see they had a choice in this matter; they could serve God or Baal. God was not going to force them to serve Him and Satan had no power to force them to serve Baal.

Christ gives a choice to serve him as well. We can either choose the "Salvation Way" or reject it. It is either the "way of rest" or "way to destruction". Again, He does not force us, and Satan cannot force us either.

Jesus did not force anyone to come to Him. Even though He offered eternal life, many chose not to accept it.

As seen in Matthew 23:37, Christ was ready to bless Jerusalem, including all the Jews, and they were not forced to do so, nor could Satan stop it, yet they refused. The Jews had a choice in this matter and were blamable.

> "The times of ignorance therefore God overlooked. But now he commands that all people everywhere should repent." Acts 17:30

No man has to follow the Devil. We are commanded to repent of our sins by God. Satan cannot keep us from following God, it is *our* choice.

2 Peter 3:9 tells us that God is always ready for us to repent and live for him, however he will never force us. There are not devils enough on this earth or in hell to keep us from repenting if we choose to do so.

Scripture proves that there are two ways, LIFE and DEATH or GOOD and EVIL. So if a person is lost, who is to blame for it? Is God? Is Satan? God gives us FREE WILL, so obviously WE ARE BLAMABLE!

IS SATAN RESPONSIBLE FOR HUMAN SIN? (1 Corinthians 10:13)

God's Plan deems it necessary that we be tempted and tested by the Evil One. However, this verse plainly teaches that he will NEVER ALLOW THE DEVIL TO TEMPT US BEYOND OUR ABILITY TO RESIST Satan. He always provides a Way of Escape. Therefore, if we sin, the Devil is not blamable, as WE are guilty for not doing our part to resist the sin. We cannot blame Satan or even God, since we had the choice to "flee from sin" and chose not to.

IS THE DEVIL BLAMABLE FOR OUR SPIRITUAL DEATH? (Romans 5:12)

Satan is not responsible for sin entering this world. It was entered by man, as this verse plainly teaches. Satan did deceive and tempt Eve in the Garden of Eden. But, the Devil did not force her to yield to this temptation. Even then, God had provided her the strength and endurance to overcome being tempted. Sin entered the world by man, not Satan. He failed to use his God-given strength to yield to Satan's temptation. The Fall of Man was caused by man himself, not Satan or any other being. Man is responsible for sin and spiritual death. God had furnished man all the needed information about the "Tree of Death" in Eden, but he and Eve yielded to Satan's temptation, thus man brought about his own "earthly punishment".

CAN GOD EVER BE BLAMED FOR SIN IN THIS WORLD? (James 1:13)

God's eternal plan calls for Satan to test man in every possible way, but man does not have to yield to his temptations. As we see in the above verse, God will *never* tempt anyone with evil.

Since God does not tempt with evil and always provides a way of escape when Satan tempts us, and will not allow the test to be greater than we can bear, then it becomes clear that the Devil himself is not responsible for human sin and suffering, death and destructions and certainly God is not, then who is? I believe that we have already answered this question, man is. The Trinity, God, Christ, and the Holy Spirit, plus every good thing, make up our Tree of Life. On the other hand, Satan and all unrighteousness represent the Tree of Death. We are not forced by God to partake of the Living Tree. Neither does Satan have the power to compel any of us to partake of the Death Tree. Therefore, man can make the choice through his own free will. If he chooses death, then *he alone* is responsible. He cannot blame God or the Devil, but only himself, as God has always given man a way for escape.

This choice can be compared to an election. God votes for all people to be saved. Satan votes for all to be lost. THE WAY THAT MAN VOTES WILL DECIDE THE ELECTION. If he is lost, it is the result of *his own vote*. Neither God nor Satan is responsible.

Chapter 17

WHERE DID SATAN COME FROM

No one really knows when Satan came into being. However, the Bible contains Scriptures that point to his origin, and they can be easily overlooked.

A strong case has been made that Satan never resided in, or "fell from God's heaven", as God hates sin and would never allow it, death, or any wars to happen up there.

Presented here are three Scriptures, which, if taken together, may prove when Satan originated.

SIN ENTERED THE WORLD BY MAN, NOT SATAN. (Romans 5:12)

There was no sin in this world until it was entered by man. There was no "being" back of man who sinned. Next will be a second suggestion that, when taken together, will more clearly show his entry into the world.

DID SATAN SIN FROM THE BEGINNING, NOT MAN? (1 John 3:8; John 8:44)

In Romans 5:12, we learned that sin entered man, and that man was here on the earth when sin appeared. In John 8:44 and 1 John 3:8, it is revealed that the "Devil sinned from the beginning", showing that sin did not precede man, neither did the Devil. Scriptures plainly mean that the Devil sinned from the time of his own "beginning". The Devil never existed in some period when he was not a "sinner", as so many have taught—taught by those who believe he was in that Heaven up yonder. Since sin came by man, when the Devil tempted man, it makes all sin, that of the Devil and that of man, starting with the "Fall of Man" in Eden.

The "Devil sinned from the beginning" and "he was a liar from the beginning". He began his lying to man in Eden; there was no lying prior to that time. He began his sinning then and there, as Eden was his "beginning". Prior to man, there was no sinning, since "by one man sin entered the world." Thus, we had no period of sin prior to man. If sin existed, "sin did not enter by man." This would be contrary to Scripture. Therefore, Satan had to originate at the time that God created man.

SATAN WAS CLASSIFIED AS A BEAST THAT GOD CREATED. (Genesis 3:1)

Genesis 3:1 does not plainly show that God made the Devil, but he is certainly pointed out to be different from the other beasts of creation. Why would God speak of the "serpent" if he were not one of the "creatures" that He made?

Thus far, Scripture reveals that Satan sinned from the beginning, from "his own beginning", as well as the creation of man, and sin entered this world by man at this time. Therefore, the origin of the Devil does not begin before man, as the Devil "did not fall to this earth" from God's heavenly home.

When man was created, God's plan made it necessary that there should be a "tempter" to test him in all possible ways, and it was at that time that Satan came into existence.

Sin did not originate in God's heavenly home, as God hates sin and would never allow it there. Sin originated with man and there was no sin prior to him, neither was there a devil before the creation of man.

Chapter 18

SEVEN TREES OF LIFE

If you are a student of the Bible, you already know about the Tree of Life that God created in the Garden of Eden. But, did you know that there are six other trees of life recorded in Scripture?

THE TREE OF LIFE IN THE GARDEN OF EDEN. (Genesis 2:9)

There is a bizarre history surrounding this "Eden Tree of Life." It was located in the center of the Garden, and right beside it was the "Death Tree". There is no documented history that Adam or Eve ever touched or tasted fruit of the Living Tree. Why didn't they? That is the question. Certainly, Adam and Eve would have "lived forever" had they not sinned in the Garden, as God's original plan was immortality for them and humanity.

Through the ages, Eve has been totally blamed for her mistake. In 1 Timothy 2:14, Paul writes that she was the object of pity:

> "Adam wasn't deceived, but the woman, being deceived, has fallen into disobedience."

This verse clearly states that the woman was led to sin by deceit. Satan tricked her into believing that if she picked and ate the fruit of the Living Tree, she would not die. He assured her that her eyes would be opened and she would become like a god, knowing good from evil. She knew God and had seen Him, and the thought of becoming like Him was more than she could resist. The Devil did not deceive her through the ignorance of God's law, for she quoted that verbatim to the Devil. It would seem that Eve was overwhelmed with the thought that being like God was the greatest value possible for herself and Adam. She was like a child, wanting to be just like her father. Therefore, when she ate the fruit, it was not to be malicious or to disobey God, she just wanted to be like Him, to become the greatest woman that could be produced. We see in 1 John 3:2, that Christ, like the Devil, set forth the same goal to his followers:

> "Beloved, now we are children of God, and it is not yet revealed what we will be. But we know that, when he is revealed, we will be like him; for we will see him just as he is."

The promise here is that we would be like Him and have the likeness of God which is the very thing Satan was promising Eve. This goal that he promised her was a good one, just the way to reach it would be the problem for all mankind. The method that Satan used was to disobey God's Word and use another method of approach.

The question now would be: Why would God not

forgive this "first sin", as it was committed through the Devil's deception and not willfully? Some may say: God did not forgive them, as He gave a strong warning that she and Adam were to die the day they ate this forbidden fruit! However, there were times in the Bible where God relented, and did not do what He said He would do.

For example, in the book of Jonah, God said Nineveh would fall in forty days, but changed his mind.

If He changed his mind about destroying Nineveh, why did he not have mercy on Eve in the Garden? It would seem out of character that the God of love, the God who taught us through Jesus Christ to forgive seventy times seven (Matthew 18:21-22), would not forgive Eve's mistake, the first ever in the world. After all, God was their Father, and they his first two adult children. They had never disobeyed Him before. This time, they were deceived, and were hoping to be just like their own Father, and seemingly, at first, He showed not the least bit of mercy. Does that seem odd that God would treat them like that? Well, He did and that would not be all.

There in the garden, the medicine Adam and Eve needed, the "balm of Gilead" was right there for the taking. It would cure what they needed for their sin and dying.

In Genesis 3:22-23, God explains that even though they had eaten of the forbidden fruit, man could still live forever. If he would only eat of the Tree of Life, that could be the remedy for man's fall there in Eden. Instead, God's Plan for removal of ALL sin became necessary much later through Christ's shed blood on the cross of Calvary. So why was it that a gracious God of love, of boundless mercy, would not allow them to use this remedy? Why was it when Adam and Eve did not want to leave their home in the Garden, but wanted to start all over again, that God "drove" them out (Genesis 3:24)?

Was this the same God that later "so loved the world that He gave His Only Son to die for our sins?" It doesn't seem like it, does it? But, He was and has always been the same God.

Like we see earthly parents, it seems that a good, kind, loving father would understand their first mistake and call his children to him, having pity for their disobedience. Would he not assure them that his confidence in his children was unshaken, that they would be more careful next time, not to allow the Devil to deceive them again? Then, to reverse His decision, He would have immediately sent them to the Tree of Life, urging them to eat of it and have everlasting life. In our minds, we would imagine that any good earthly parent would have done it that way.

God has so much more love than that, much more kindness and grace that He manifested by not allowing Adam and Eve to remain in Eden, sending them away from the Tree of Life of Divine planting. God never makes a mistake. He never abuses one of His children. He never does anything except the very "best" for any one. His Eternal Plan is far better than a "Garden of Eden" on this earth.

FIELD TREE OF LIFE. (Deuteronomy 20:19-20)
The "Field Tree" is the earthly or natural "tree of life."

WISDOM TREE OF LIFE. (Proverbs 3:18)

FRUIT OF RIGHTEOUSNESS TREE OF LIFE. (Proverbs 11:30)

DESIRE TREE OF LIFE. (Proverbs 13:12)

TONGUE TREE OF LIFE. (Proverbs 15:4)

CHRIST TREE OF LIFE. (Revelation 22:2)

We have come from the "Tree of Life" in the Garden of Eden to the Christ Tree of Life. While in the Garden, man had a perfect world. Then, Satan tempted Eve with the fruit from that Tree of Life, she tasted it, and we know the rest of the story. God had given them "free will" and the Devil had his opportunity for the "first temptation of man". Satan did not force Eve to eat, thus the first great sin came about through her weakness and willingness to succumb to "the serpent"!

Since God knew that man would fall, he already had a plan of salvation in place bringing us to the "Christ Tree of Life." Christ is the great "Tree of Life" and the greatest Living Tree this world has ever known.

> "And the God of peace will quickly crush Satan under your feet. The grace of our Lord Jesus Christ be with you." (Romans 16:20)

Satan will have completed his role in the eternal plan. On that final Day of Judgment, he will be "crushed under the feet of the Lord.

Chapter 19

VICTORY OVER SATAN—SALVATION

Throughout this book, Scripture reveals Satan as the enemy of man from his first appearance in the Garden of Eden until this very moment. However, his evil influence upon this earth will end on judgment day when he, his demons and all unbelievers will be cast into hell, that bottomless pit full of fire and brimstone, where they will suffer unspeakable punishment for eternity!

To avoid that horrendous fate, this chapter offers hope for Christians: An eternal home in heaven where unimaginable bliss and joy is awaiting those on judgment day who have put on Christ in baptism, being added to His Church, and remained faithful to God, Christ, and the Holy Spirit while here on this earth!

God sent His Son, Jesus Christ, to this earth as a needed Savior for mankind. For this purpose, *Christ would establish His Church,* as recorded in the book of Acts.

Now when Jesus came into the parts of Caesarea

Philippi, He asked his disciples, saying, "Who do men say that I, the Son of Man, am?"

In Matthew 16:13-18, Jesus plainly tells his disciples and the world that *HE CHOSE to establish HIS ONE and ONLY CHURCH and it shall stand for eternity!*

CAN WE THEN ATTEND THE CHURCH OF *OUR* CHOICE?

When we travel across this great land by automobile, many times we see a sign upon entering a city that reads, "Attend the Church of Your Choice". It will list each "church denomination" in that community, be it Baptist, Methodist, Presbyterian, Nazarene, Lutheran, Episcopal, Catholic, or other places of worship. Have you ever wondered why there are so many "churches?" *Which one do we choose…or can we?* If so, *which one of these is the right church?*

According to David Barrett, editor of the World Christian Encyclopedia, a comparative survey of churches and religions (AD 33 to Present Day) shows there are nineteen major world religions, which are subdivided into a total of 270 large religious groups, along with many smaller ones.

Scripture tells us that Heaven *will NOT be crowded!*

> Jesus said: "Enter through the narrow gate. For *wide* is the gate and *broad* is the road *that leads to destruction,* and *many enter through it.* But *small* is the gate and *narrow* the road that *leads to life* and *only a few find it."* (Matthew 7:13-14)

So, which *church* offers the *"small gate and narrow road"* that leads to salvation?

> Not everyone who says to me, 'Lord, Lord,' will enter into the Kingdom of Heaven; but *he who does the will* of my Father who is in heaven. Many will tell me in that day, 'Lord, Lord, didn't we prophesy in your name, in your name cast out demons, and in your name do many mighty works?' Then I will tell them, '*I never knew you. Depart from me, you who work iniquity.*' (Matthew 7:21-23)
>
> You hypocrites! Well did Isaiah prophesy of you, saying, 'These people draw near to me with their mouth, and honor me with their lips; but their heart is far from me. And *in vain do they worship me*, teaching as doctrine, *rules made by men.*' (Matthew 15:7-9)

Likewise,

> "There is a way which seems right to a man, but in the end *it leads to death.*" (Proverbs 14:12)

THERE IS ONLY *ONE* CHOICE LEADING TO THAT 'NARROW ROAD' TO HEAVEN!

In Ephesians 4:4-6, the Apostle Paul teaches us:

> "There is *one* body and *one* Spirit, even as you also were called in *one* hope of your calling; *one* Lord, *one* faith, *one* baptism; *one* God and Father of all, who is over all and through all and in us all."

The apostle Paul appeals to the church at Corinth in 1 Corinthians 1:10...

> "Now I beg you, brothers, through the name of our Lord, Jesus Christ, that *you all speak the same thing* and that there be *no divisions among you*, but that you *be perfected together in the same mind* and *in the same judgment.*"

In John 14:6, Jesus tells us:

> "I am the way, the truth, and the life. NO ONE comes to the Father, except through ME."

These verses teach us that there is *only one* "small gate to that narrow road that leads to salvation!" Would you not agree, these verses alone, eliminate any choice of all *modern*-day *denominations, man-inspired religions* and *"isms"?*

The Bible identifies only *one* church...
- o The Body of Christ (Colossians 1:18)
- o The Bride of Christ (Ephesians 5:22-27)
- o The Family of God (I Timothy 3:15)
- o The Pillar and Ground of Truth (1 Timothy 3:15)

The Founder (*Christ,* not man)...
- o Jesus promised to build HIS church (Matthew 16:18)
- o Jesus purchased the church with HIS blood (Acts 20:28)
- o Jesus is the HEAD of the church (Colossians 1:18)
- o The church is HIS spiritual body (Colossians 1:18)

The Establishment of the church...
- o It was promised in the last days of Jerusalem (Isaiah 2:2-4)
- o The church was near in John's day (Matthew 3:1-2)
- o Jesus told His disciples that they should not taste of death till they see the kingdom of God come with power (Mark 9:1)
- o They were told that they would receive that power when the Holy Spirit came upon them (Acts 1:8)
- o All these things came to pass on Pentecost (Acts 2)

Names of the church...
- The church of the Lord (Acts 20:28)
- The church of God (1 Corinthians 1:1-2)
- The body of Christ (Ephesians 4:12)
- The church of Christ (Romans 16:16)

The word "church" comes from the Greek word which means those "called out". It does not refer to the "building" where Christians meet, but to the *"people"* who meet there.

Church can also correctly be translated to the *"assembly" or "assembled"*.

The church offers mankind...
- Forgiveness of sins is in the church (Ephesians 1:17)
- Salvation is in the church (2 Timothy 2:10)
- Redemption is in the church (Colossians 1:14)
- All Spiritual blessings are in the church (Ephesians 1:3)

Scripture gives us very simple directions to this *"narrow road"* that leads to SALVATION...

GOD'S PLAN OF SALVATION
- HEAR the Gospel. (Romans 10:14)
- BELIEVE that Jesus Christ is your Lord and Savior. (Hebrews 11:6)
- REPENT of your past sins. (Acts 17:30)
- CONFESS Jesus as Lord. (Acts 8:36-37)
- BAPTIZE for the forgiveness of sins. (Acts 2:38)
- LIVE a Christian life. (1 Peter 2:9; Philippians 2:12)

ALL of the above complete a *"chain of simple steps"* that are REQUIRED to become a Christian.

Here are more Scripture references that clearly define God's Plan of Salvation.

HEAR the Gospel.

Matthew 7:24	Acts 15:7
Luke 6:47	Acts 18:8
Luke 11:28	Acts 19:5
Acts 4:4	Romans 10:17

BELIEVE that Jesus Christ is your Lord and Savior.

Mark 1:15	John 11:25
Mark 16:16	John 20:31
John 1:7	Acts 8:12
John 3:16	Acts 8:13
John 3:18	Acts 10:43
John 3:36	Acts 13:39
John 5:24	Acts 16:31
John 6:35	Romans 1:16
John 6:40	Romans 10:9
John 6:47	1 John 3:23
John 8:24	1 John 5:13

REPENT of your past sins.

Matthew 4:17	Acts 2:38
Mark 1:15	Acts 3:19
Mark 6:12	Acts 8:22
Luke 13:3	Revelation 2:5
Luke 15:7	Revelation 3:19

CONFESS Jesus as Lord.

Matthew 10:32	Luke 12:8

Romans 10:9	1 John 2:23
Romans 10:10	1 John 4:15
1 Timothy 6:12	Revelation 3:5

BAPTIZE for the forgiveness of sins, becoming a member of the Lord's Body, His church.

Mark 16:16	Acts 10:48
Acts 2:41	Acts 16:33
Acts 8:12	Acts 18:8
Acts 8:13	Acts 19:5
Acts 8:36	Acts 22:16
Acts 8:38	Romans 6:3
Acts 9:18	Galatians 3:27
Acts 10:47	1 Corinthians 12:13

Scriptures prove that baptism is *required* for our salvation. Of course, we must first *believe*. (1 Peter 3:20-21).

At the moment of coming up out of the water of baptism, we are added to the Church *Body of Christ* and only then can we wear the name of Christian (Acts 11:26).

John 3:16 is one of the most frequently quoted Scriptures today for salvation. This verse is certainly true. However, the act of being saved is *more* than just accepting Christ into our hearts or 'faith only', as taught by many.

Those who profess 'faith only salvation' point to the thief hanging on the cross next to Jesus as being saved by his confession of faith, without baptism. I submit there are three reasons why Jesus told the thief, *"Today, you will be with me in paradise."*

    1. New Testament Scripture clearly proves that baptism is the final requirement in the plan of

salvation. By definition, a testament (a will) is *not* in effect until *after* the testator dies. Obviously, Jesus was still alive on the cross when he pardoned the thief, thus the New Testament *baptism as a requirement for salvation* was *not* yet in effect.

2. Even though Jesus died before him, the thief was in no position to be baptized, as he was nailed to the cross.

3. And most importantly, God can save anyone he chooses. It is not up to us to question His judgment. We are simply commanded to obey His Word.

First and foremost, we must believe that the Bible is the infallible Word of God. With any biblical subject, Scripture must be studied in *full context,* not just "pick and choose verses" to prove what *we want to believe,* but the *truth* on any subject.

> "Because the foolishness of God is wiser than men, and the weakness of God is stronger than men." (1 Corinthians 1:25)

When we talk to or teach others about salvation, it must be understood that it is *not* what *we* say, but what the *Word of God* says. We should never be self-righteous!

WHAT ABOUT INFANT BAPTISM...IS IT ALSO REQUIRED?

The baptism of a baby is viewed by many as a special event not only for the parents, but grandparents and other interested relatives and friends. A baptismal dress is purchased, and photographs are taken. The baby certainly does not like being sprinkled on the head by a robed priest or clergyman at a church building and lets everyone know about it. The little white dress is stored away as a sentimental keepsake.

You may be reading of this ritual and may have been baptized yourself as an infant. Then your question may be...Why then are babies being baptized? We will see what the Bible teaches us about this event.

Let's first discuss the Catholic view on this subject. It is based on the idea that babies are born into "original sin", that is the fall of Adam and Eve in the Garden of Eden. In the Catholic Church, adult baptism is performed for the remission of sins, and according to their belief, it should be included for infants as well. Pope Clement IV declared in 1267 that infants who die without baptism die in their original sins and are excluded from the vision of God. The doctrine of "Limbo", the intermediate state between the suffering in hell and glory of heaven, was implemented to satisfy grieving mothers whose children died without baptism.

The Old Testament book of Ezekiel is very clear on the subject of the son *not* inheriting the sins of his father. In Chapter 18, verse 20, God is talking to the Israelites, as well as all of mankind, when he says, "the son shall not bear the iniquity *sins* of his father, neither shall the father bear the iniquity of his son." Both the father and the son will give an account for *their own sins* on the day of judgment! All of Chapter 18 leaves no doubt on this issue. Refer also to Deuteronomy 24:16.

For most Protestants, infant baptism is not considered a matter of salvation. Generally, Protestants who believe in salvation by faith only would not accept infant baptism as necessary for salvation anyway. Those who do baptize their babies do so as a promise that the parents will raise their child in a godly home and bring him or her to church services. Scripture does teach that parents are to raise their children from infancy in the *"discipline* and *instruction* of the Lord" (Ephesians 6:4).

Some use the Scriptures to justify baptizing infants from the New Testament accounts of whole families or "households" being baptized. Thus, this thinking would also include babies. (See Acts 11:14; Acts 16:15; Acts 16:33; Acts 18:8; 1 Corinthians 1:16.) However, there is no Scripture which teaches that babies inherit sin from Adam or their parents. There is *no requirement* for infant baptism taught in the Bible.

Remember, the plan of salvation plainly teaches that one must first *hear the Word, believe in Christ, repent of sins,* and *confess Jesus as the Son of God*...And then be *baptized for the remission of sins.* Obviously, a baby does not have this capability. All Biblical accounts of a baptism involve "immersion in water", *not* sprinkling of water on the head.

If baptism is not required for infants, then at what age do young people need to do that? This will vary among individuals, but it is widely held within the church that it is required at the *"age of accountability"*. This means that whenever a young person knows the difference between right and wrong (sinful behavior), this would be the age when they should consider being baptized into Christ to become a Christian. There is no set age or time, as this depends on the maturity level of the boy or girl.

HOW DOES A CHRISTIAN WORSHIP GOD?

God's Word gives us very simple and specific instructions as to how he wants us to worship Him. (John 4:23-24)

Meet Together

We are to meet together *on the first day of the week, Sunday,* and do so at every opportunity that we may have. (Hebrews 10:24-25)

Singing

We are to praise God through singing. From all indications, the Bible teaches that Christians are to sing *"a cappella"*, which means without the use of instrumental music. Scripture does not specifically say that we can or cannot use music in worship; however, the position of the church should always be, *"when in doubt, do without"*. God's wrath will be severe on those who would *"add to"* or *"take away from"* His perfect Will! After all, it is *not* about us, but always pleasing God in *all* that we do for Him! (Ephesians 5:17, 19; Acts 16:25)

Pray

In our public worship service, the man is to lead, while the rest of the congregation listens and prays silently, giving thanks and praise to God. (Philippians 4:6, Daniel 4:34)

When we pray to God the Father, both public and private, we are to pray through Jesus' name for God to hear our prayers. Jesus is our Advocate with the Father. A prayer should not be ended with a simple Amen.

Rather, *"In the name of Christ we pray"* or *"name of Jesus we pray, Amen."* (1 John 2:1; Colossians 3:17.)

Lord's Supper

Christians are to partake of the Lord's Supper on *each first day of the week, Sunday.* This is not a common meal, but a memorial supper consisting of "breaking" of unleavened bread, representing *Christ's body* which was sacrificed by his death on the cross. The "fruit of the vine", or grape juice, represents his shed blood on the cross. (Acts 20:7; 1 Corinthians 10:16-17)

Offering

Worship service also includes a convenient time for the giving back to God. The purpose is to provide financial means to carry on the work of the church. This would include financially supporting a preacher; buying and maintaining a building (meeting place); funds for benevolence, be it for church members, especially widows or others who may be in immediate need; and, most importantly, financial support for the congregation to *"spread the Gospel"* to others in the community or wherever they may have an opportunity (1 Corinthians 16:1-2). There is no mention of "tithing" or giving 10 percent of your income being required in the New Testament, as it was under the Old Law.

Preaching

In order to obey the Gospel, one must hear God's Word preached, which must be part of any worship service.

This is the greatest commandment of Christ: *preaching* and *teaching* the Gospel of Salvation each and every opportunity that a Christian may have. (Mark 16:15-16.)

Why is it so important in our spiritual lives while here on this earth that we follow God's Word to the best of our ability in all things that we do, including obeying and teaching the plan of salvation, worshiping Him and living a Christian life?

God makes it very clear in Scripture that He will *not* tolerate our changing of His Word to suit *our own* beliefs or teachings. His *severe warning* is mentioned three times, in the beginning, middle, and last few verses of the Bible (Deuteronomy 4:2; Proverbs 30:5-6; Revelation 22:18-19).

Scripture reveals Satan as the enemy of man from his first appearance in the Garden of Eden until this very moment. However, his evil influence upon this earth will end on judgment day when he, his demons and *all* unbelievers will be cast into hell, that bottomless pit full of fire and brimstone, where they will suffer unspeakable punishment for eternity! (Ephesians 6:10-17; 1 Corinthians 15:54-58.)

We, as Christians, can avoid that horrendous fate with the *hope* that we have through the shed blood of Jesus Christ. There is an eternal home in heaven where unimaginable bliss and joy is awaiting those on judgment day who have *put on Christ in baptism, been added to His Church* and *remained faithful to God, Christ,* and *the Holy Spirit* while we are here on this earth!

After reading The Plan of Salvation, let me ask you...Are you truly a born-again Christian, washed in the blood of the Lamb, our Savior, Jesus Christ, thus being added to His *one and only* CHURCH?

It is not what I have said in this book, but what GOD'S WORD tells you about the *most important event in your life!*

If there is any doubt at all in where you hope to spend eternity, I implore you to study *The Plan of Salvation* in your Bible and pray for God, through the Holy Spirit, to show you that "Narrow Road" leading to Heaven. Becoming a TRUE CHRISTIAN is *the most important decision that you will ever make!*

YOU CANNOT AFFORD TO WAIT.
NONE OF US ARE PROMISED A TOMORROW!

DO IT TODAY!

GOD BLESS

WHO IS JOHN KARSTETTER?

John graduated as an honor student from Cameron University in Lawton, Oklahoma, earning an Associate of Science degree in Law Enforcement (1972) and Bachelor of Science in Business (1973). Upon entering the corporate world, he enjoyed a successful career in sales and marketing, semi-retiring in 2010.

Today, he has returned to his second career as a Licensed Private Detective, specializing in Public and Government Investigations, Church Security Training, Executive Protection and Workplace Violence Assessment/Training.

He is an NRA Certified Firearms Instructor/Chief Range Safety Officer, and a Certified Kansas/Missouri Concealed Carry Handgun Instructor. John is a Member of Concealed Advantage, a Network of Highly Trained Missouri/Kansas Firearms Instructors, each operating their own business. He teaches other firearms training courses, including NRA Basic Pistol Shooting, Teenager and Women's Gun Safety, and The New FBI Shooting Qualifications Course.

Speaking of the Devil is John's second book. His first, *Nutrition Guidelines,* was a product instruction manual for alternate healthcare products, selling over 25,000 copies. His writing skills were developed during his college years, through experience with advertising campaigns, written presentations and press releases in the corporate world, along with the narrative writing style required for his own P.I. field investigation reports.

John and his wife, Jana, have two sons and a daughter-in-law. He serves as deacon at 151st Street Church of Christ in Olathe, Kansas.